TRAILER TRASH

an '80s Memoir

ANGIE CAVALLARI

Trailer Trash: an '80s Memoir

Copyright © 2018 by Retro Publishing, LLC. All Rights Reserved.

For information about this title or to order other books and/or electronic media, contact the publisher:
Retro Publishing, LLC
Denver, Colorado
RetroPublishingLLC@gmail.com

Library of Congress Control Number: 2018950993

ISBNs: 978-1-7324618-0-2 (softcover)
978-1-7324618-1-9 (eBook)

Printed in the United States of America

Cover and Interior design: 1106 Design

Publisher's Cataloging-In-Publication Data in process

*To Grey and Sage who have opened
and filled so many unexplored
places in my heart and continue to
inspire me each day. I love you.*

Contents

Introduction

N THE CHURCH PEWS, I sit and rise in agitated but familiar discomfort. I am realizing little has changed since my childhood and the practice of religion is still very unorthodox to me in spite of years of practice and ritual. I'm going through the motions when I had the epiphany that my bizarre childhood would make for a better book than the last ten or twelve novels that I had stopped and started throughout my adult life. Call it divine intervention but my discernment at that moment was fitting considering that I attended prestigious parochial schools while being raised in a run-down shit hole kind of trailer park sometimes thirty miles away in distance and always worlds away from my home life. The bitterness of my upbringing has always been distracted by the fact that I was lucky enough to grow up in the 1980s and under the presence and guidance of my eccentric, and wealthy Grandmother. Still, my Mother's airs were never allowed to fly due to Grandma's propensity for donning crudely cut-off denim shorts, halter tops with no bra and t-shirts brandishing support of Ronald Reagan and Oliver North. Three responsive readings and a doxology later and I had sketched out my entire chapter outline on the worship bulletin. I'm looking over at my husband who's giving me the same judgmental eye I had experienced whenever my school staff reminded me of my place in society and that my parents really needed Jesus because my mom wore bikinis and my dad listened to The Rolling Stones.This was my life and I think 1980s Jesus would certainly approve of the profanity, nostalgia and the story and lesson that lies within the pages of this book.

CHAPTER 1

Owner's Manual

TRAILER-PARK OWNERS never use the word "trailer" and certainly not the term "trailer park."

At some point in time, even the Mobile Home Park Owners Association (MHPOA for short) realized that the word "trailer" had a negative connotation. When was the last time you saw a "trailer park community" advertised on TV?

"Trailer park" has come to represent, in the minds of most Americans, men in stained work shirts dotted with drippings of food fat and car excrement returning home to take out life's shortcomings on the innocents in their lives—the ol' lady, the dog, and the coffee table.

This image—which, I can tell you, is a partially true cliché in our society—vaguely explains why my parents and my grandparents decided to rent to tenants without children or pets. Well, birds and rodents were deemed acceptable but not guinea pigs. Guinea pigs, due to size and temperament, were completely unacceptable.

Before moving forward, you will want to familiarize yourself with some mobile-home-park-owner's lingo.

Mobile Home—Under no circumstances was the word "trailer" to be in used if you were in the mobile-home-park business.

TPD—Tampa Police Department: the acronym that represented the exhausted members of law enforcement who never backed down from the call to mitigate those aforementioned shortcomings, violence, or rusted-out stoops.

Tenants—Term for the people who rented mobile homes. Tenants had many rental terms to choose from, including weekly or even monthly, based on their credit, which was either nonexistent or downright shitty.

Lot Number—Typically, each mobile home was owned by the landlords and sat on a lot, to which a number was assigned by the landlords. However, if the lot was empty, it did occasionally happen that the tenants would pull up in a burned-out Winnebago and rent just the lot itself. Lot numbers were assigned to the tenants' mobile-home space rather than an actual address.

The Park—The nickname often used by owners of mobile-home parks. As the years went by, this term was uttered in disgust, the same way profanity was used when no other word would do.

Lot Rent—Monies collected on a weekly or monthly basis in the form of cash or check only. Credit cards were never accepted, and most of the tenants didn't have the kind

of jobs to afford what Telly Savalas was
hawking.

MHP—Acronym for "Mobile Home Park."

Eviction—Also known as "kicking out the tenants," this process was considered a big pain
in the ass. After spending at least sixty days
without collecting squat from the tenants,
MHP owners would take the legal means
necessary to remove tenants from their rented
mobile homes. No one liked this process.
It was time consuming and stressful, and it
usually resulted in the tenant showing up at
the front door, threatening violence. In their
defense, these are people who were frankly
ill-prepared to handle life or who had just
opted out of it entirely.

My name is Angie Cavallari, and this is my story
about growing up as an '80s child in the shitty, impov-
erished, modern-age ghettos known as trailer parks.

CHAPTER 2

Life Begins at Ninety Degrees

1980

MY MOTHER HATED being cold. Whenever the temperature dropped below eighty-seven degrees Fahrenheit, she'd commit to a wardrobe of heavily woven wool garments—and she was not shy about dressing like this even indoors. Her personal insulation project extended to her offspring as well, and I, along with my brother and sister, was bundled to the point that mobility was not possible.

In her defense, Chicago was no place for someone like my mother, who has been cold her entire life. My parents were both Chicago natives, and my dad, who seemed to be better acclimated to climate and change in general, was allowed to wear whatever he wanted.

I loved how my father dressed. He looked like an Italian mobster right out of the film *The Godfather.* Unlike his childhood friends who ended up doing manual labor in the then-thriving steel mills of the 1960s and early 1970s, who were required to don thermal jumpsuits, my father sported a long, leather trench coat complemented with a thick, luxurious mustache. In fact, my father's mustache and stature ruined any sexual attraction I could have ever had to my favorite tropical television sleuth, Magnum P.I.

Standing at more than six feet three inches tall, with broad shoulders, he spent his day in the offices of Inland Steel ferrying executives around in shiny automobiles the size of modern-day land barges that, today, could squeeze only into those parking spaces reserved for buses and Winnebagos.

He loved his job, but my mom hated the Chicago weather. So, following the brutal and historic blizzard of 1979, we traded in our Chevelle SS for a 1977 Dodge van.

In January of 1980, we loaded up our new family truckster, affectionately known as *The Brick,* and followed our U-Haul and my mother's dreams of dripping sweat year-round to sunny 2251 Pelican Lane in Tampa, Florida.

The Brick was dark maroon, had wall-to-wall carpeting to match, two captains' chairs, a sink/fridge combo, a plush sofa, and the strong scent of mildew, thanks to a small leak that had sprung in the sunroof and had, on many occasions, saturated the tightly woven carpet fibers.

It also lacked seatbelts, which was common at the time; they were not required by law. For many years, my grandma had a bumper sticker on her brown Ford F-150 that read, "I'll buckle up when Bundy does." This was intended as a statement about fighting the passage of seat-belt laws in Florida, in recognition of the many times that Florida serial killer Ted Bundy managed to escape execution by electricity.

My favorite spot while traveling was with my back to the windshield, sitting on the large plastic console that separated the two captain's chairs between the driver and front passenger seats. You couldn't stay parked there too long, as the console doubled as an engine cover, and the heat would come on so suddenly you would be sent to the back sofa with third-degree burns.

The Brick had its original eight-track player, and, in 1980, my parents popped for the additional and state-of-the-art tape deck. However, cassette tapes were still in their infancy, and so most of the music we listened to while making the drive down Interstate 75 was part of the eight-track collection. "Minute by Minute," by the Doobie Brothers, was playing in time to the rhythm of windshield wipers as rain instead of January snow fell hard upon *The Brick*. Many of my childhood memories are strongly tied to shag rugs, the pungent aroma of mildew, and Yacht Rock.

My grandparents had already moved to Tampa two years earlier and set up shop collecting lot rents and evicting tenants. The mobile home park was called "Placid Lakes." However, the only lake on the property was Grandma's community pool and the occasional flooding due to a poor drainage system and Florida's heavy downpours. Grandma never cared for the irony of the name but never bothered with the expense of making any changes. She loved the emotional and financial benefits of frugality. Overall, Grandma and Papa were enjoying the success of entrepreneurship in the MHP industry and sold my parents on the lucrative benefits of mobile-home-park ownership in Florida.

Turning onto Pelican Avenue, I couldn't help but notice the large parking lot and medieval-inspired building next door to our new home and mobile home park. Large, dirty stained-glass windows shielded the shame of what might be happening inside before the noon hour. A group of adults appeared to be forming a semicircle around a tanned and extremely overweight man sitting on a black pleather barstool that doubled as a doorstop. They were shielding their eyes from the midmorning sun and cigarette smoke, which created the appearance of an almost-mystic haze swirling around their huddle.

It reminded me of the motel we had stayed in on our way to Florida. It was called The Knights Inn and was themed—both inside and out—like a castle, including purple velveteen curtains and bedspreads, all fit for royalty. The only thing missing was Merlin, his trusty owl, and a large caldron where spells and potions could be concocted. At the mobile-home park, I begged to go inside this new, mysterious establishment, but my parents assured me that five-year-olds were not welcome because they didn't serve Shirley

Temples. I later learned that this place was a bar called "Godfather's Lounge," but the sign was way past the point of legibility and, like its patrons, was a shadow of its former self. Still, it appealed to me because it was within stumbling distance of our backyard.

At the entrance to the park sat a white duplex with a dilapidated sign in the front yard that read, "Pelican Mobile Home Park." Unlike "Godfather's," the letters were hanging on for life and could still spell out the business name. This was it—our new home. Surrounding our new digs were mobile homes that appeared to have been manufactured in the 1960s, painted in faded hues of pink and turquoise. These modern-day tenements were crammed onto a postage-stamp-sized yard surrounding a gravel horseshoe road.

There was no running into our cinder-block castle and claiming a room as our own. This was because our house was still occupied, with tenants on the other side of the wall. We would spend the next three months kicking out our very first tenants and, later, the physical wall that once separated us.

I am still not all that familiar with the process of building a duplex, but from living in one formerly, I can tell you that there are many separate interior and exterior doors, and random sinks—*everywhere*. It was decided that I would share a bedroom with my sister and that my little brother would have his own room. For the time being, we all piled into the same bedroom, with my parents in the cramped living quarters.

The difference in temperature was the first and most obvious change from living in Chicago. We had just left snow and ice and ended up in toasty temperatures hovering around a balmy eighty-two degrees in January. My mother loved every minute of it and vowed never to run the air conditioning. To this day, I can never recall an evening when a box fan was not running in one of our open bedroom windows. The *No A/C* rule applied all year long, even during the scorching Florida heat waves and record-breaking temperatures. In order to get a decent night's sleep, you would have to open the windows and prop the box fan on top of my white plastic terrarium table, filled with wispy greenery clinging to life in its manufactured environment.

Failure to angle the table or fan would result in your spending the entire night flipping a sweat-soaked pillow just to keep from swimming in your own salt and swill. I often also fell asleep to the sound of Queen's "Another One Bites the Dust" booming out of blown speakers spilling out of Godfather's along with the riff-raff.

Just six short months after our duplex housemates had been evicted, my big sister started second grade at Mendenhall Elementary, and I was ready to start school as well. However, my mother's decision to hold me back a year in school was based on a Phyllis Schlafly letter she'd read while on the toilet—or *the library,* as she liked to refer to it. I stayed home and fought the good fight of defending the obstruction of property by my four-year-old brother on my Strawberry Shortcake apparel and dolls.

Our cinder abode had been transformed into a relatively normal-looking ranch-style house. My dad even installed an attic fan to help suck out the hot air that mingled with the cigarette smoke from my parents' and Grandma's unfiltered Pall Malls.

Also new was a faux-wood particleboard door that separated the house from the front office. This door provided some level of privacy but minimal protection, as particleboard is entirely ineffective at stopping a speeding bullet or the many other threats awaiting us in the years to come.

My father had welded the former front door shut, which, after a fresh coat of white paint, went unnoticed by any of us. The shutter-style window that faced Pelican Lane was always busy with foot and car traffic all hours of the night, most likely from Godfather's Lounge.

We didn't have to wait long for our first threat. On one particular evening—and a lucky one because my sister and I were fast asleep—my dad heard someone pulling on the former front door. The next sound was the *other* front door, which opened from our living room. My dad and his magnificent mustache were waiting for them—with a shotgun. The TPD was called, and I awoke to the sounds of police radios crackling sporadically from the kitchen—a sound that would become familiar—a weekly, recurrent event during our years living in the park.

Now, this would have been enough to give pause or consideration to living offsite, but my parents wanted to capitalize as much as possible on the park as they could. Moving off property meant that funds would have to be allocated to the suburbs or at least a safer neighborhood. But the real reason, I later deduced, was my parents' hatred for the suburbs. They were the type of Baby Boomers who felt trapped by the societal rules surrounding their upbringing, and every step away from that life was an act of control and rebellion.

CHAPTER 3

The Tenants

THE FIRST TENANT MY family met was Tom Seman. Tom lived on lot number 7, located just a mere five hundred or so yards from our gravel driveway. We quickly deduced that he was the most bold and nosiest of tenants—the kind of person who gawked the longest at traffic accidents and annoyed the hell out of first responders. Not because he cared, but merely to experience the presence of emotion and tragedy.

I don't think I need to tell you that this guy lived up to his sound-alike name or that he was a pervert of the creepiest variety. In addition to his perv status, Tom had appointed himself town crier of the park.

If you needed the latest news about a wife-beating incident, Tom had the dirt and, in most cases, a copy of the police report. You could tell that he'd been a looker in his twenties but that his sedentary lifestyle had caught up with him. He looked as if he was going to give birth to a basketball at any moment. Picture Ted Kennedy circa 1990s with an additional one hundred pounds or so around his midsection.

My dad shared a deep dislike for Tom. For starters, he lingered around our house more than any other tenant and was fond of telling me that I would have an eating disorder and battle my weight when I was a teenager—a bit heavy of a conversation for a first-grader to digest. But don't worry. I later ate those words and threw them up again in my teens. Another reason to fucking hate this guy. At least I was spared the little tidbits of information about his daily ablutions such as his ball-shaving and powdering ritual. *Those* he liked to share with my mom.

She had to have at least encouraged him by not stopping him when he described the process of powdering his junk. In all honesty, my mother was quite intelligent and starved for her own kind. In spite of his position in life, his IQ was off the charts, and she welcomed any intellectual stimulation of any kind.

I was impressed, considering the fact that Ted would have needed no less than seven mirrors and risk pulling several muscles to get a look at his scrotum beneath his basketball baby. Tom's first residence was a yellow school bus that had been converted into crude living quarters.

Before speaking any further about Tom, I would like to introduce the other tenants who lived in the park.

Florence

Perhaps the most memorable tenant I knew was Florence. And we were warned never to call her "Flo" or risk a backhand to the head. Her lot sat smack dab on the south side of our yard, and, during the eight years that she lived there, I never saw her sober.

She always seemed to be coming and going from her many trips to and from the liquor store or the local watering holes, much to my father's chagrin. You may have not heard her leave, but you always heard her return, because she would take out the metal trash cans and stray cats with her 1970s pale-blue, rusted-out Cadillac. On many occasions, my father decided to perform a more subtle intervention by filling her gas tank with water while she slept off the Colt 45.

Florence held a strange fascination for me and my sister. For starters, I could never figure out her age. She may have been in only her early sixties, but I would place her around seventy-eight in booze years. And she wasn't the kind of sweet old lady who wanted to connect with children or keep butterscotch candies in a faux crystal jar for younger guests.

Most days Florence would proudly sport a halter top sans a brassiere and briskly march across her yard in crudely trimmed cut-off jeans—her cheap flip flops flailing off her feet and her sagging breasts bouncing in cadence to her determination to find escape through a good time.

She very seldom did any kind of entertaining. But I did meet her adult daughter a couple of times. She appeared to be about my mom's age, but, unlike her mother, she looked relatively normal and often embarrassed, as if the shame and strain of their relationship was not enough to even warrant conversation with a neighbor. Trisha (my mother's best friend) later divulged that Florence would often have gentleman callers, the kind who had a lounge lizard tan and hung out at Godfather's.

Hattie

If Florence couldn't fill the role of sweet old lady, Hattie certainly had potential. Hattie was short, wore flowered housecoats, and had hair the color and consistency of a Q-tip. But it came at a price—you would have to listen to her tales from the operating table. Anything from a splinter to a paper cut could set her off, and, before you knew it, you were hearing about her latest stay in the hospital and her need for a temporary colostomy bag, which she proudly displayed in spite of my protest.

Hattie was also the reason that I learned the term "hypochondriac" before I could memorize my home phone number, thanks to my mom's vocabulary lessons. Hattie lived on lot number 10, some four or five mobile homes away—which, for me, might as well have been on the other side of the world. She had formed an attachment to my family as older people often do after they have been abandoned by their own. But there was something about her voice that had a calming, zen-like effect on me, so it was relatively easy to tune out the details. Well, unless she whipped out her colostomy bag.

On the rare occasion, Hattie's estranged—and strange—son would visit her, likely looking to borrow money or poke into her finances. You knew when he would come around because his green Mark III conversion van windows would nearly shatter from the decibels of "Hot Blooded" by Foreigner blaring from the tape deck. The guy gave me the "Stay away from Uncle Wille" sort of vibe. That same vibe haunted me, for good reason, during my years in the park.

Harry

Most of the tenants were degenerate losers, but you had to feel sorry for Harry. I'd say this guy wore a "kick me" sign his entire life. Not helping matters was his appearance. Harry's gray, tousled hair was always dirty and hung, to the detriment of his vision, over his thick, horn-rimmed glasses. I also had my suspicions that he was born without an ass. His uniform of the day was a pair of abused Wrangler jeans that unknowingly clung tenaciously to his lower back and drooped where a butt crack should have been.

Harry's lot sat directly across the street from our driveway, and Harry had tinted the windows himself with Reynolds Wrap. I know this because Harry liked to share little bits of bullshit knowledge with me and my siblings. He did it in the same way that adults often underestimate children, who also have knowledge or observation skills. He would often wander over to the park office, clutching a glass of milk with his fingertips clad in Band-Aids.

Harry would then explain to me how good milk was for my health and would do this while swaying back and forth. Apparently, his milk was fortified with vitamin D *and* vodka. I knew from the tender age of six that Harry was a dipshit drunk. Still, I felt sorry for him. In fact, my heart went out to most of the tenants from a young age. I saw them for their lot in life in spite of it being self-inflicted.

Making matters worse, the whole park did as well. Trisha also explained to me why the tips of Harry's fingers were covered in Band-Aids. Turns out, Harry would get shit-faced at a local dive bar called "The Gold

Minor"—sort of a modern-day, wild-west den of sin, which it mimicked well, from its saloon doors outside to its debauchery inside. Trisha was my mom's best friend and the girlfriend of my parents' best friend, Steve Winters, who lived on lot 17 and was a truck driver and one of only two to own a unit but rent the actual lot/land from Pelican Mobile Home Park.

I knew it well from the outside, because it sat directly across from The Family Mart, where we did our grocery shopping, and down the street from United Skates of America, where my mom hosted and I attended many birthday parties.

It also came up in adult conversation quite often on the TPD radios, and I would always open my ears for a good story. Apparently, the proprietors of this local watering hole knew more about pouring shots than hanging ceiling fans.

Harry would get so drunk that he'd throw his hands up in the air, only to have the tips of the high-spinning blades hanging from a low ceiling nearly take off his fingers. This happened on a regular basis and enough for me to notice that it happened more than once. Harry lived on lot 3, directly across the street from our driveway.

Gary

Gary loved two things: cockatiels and Hamm's beer. You could say his full-time job consisted of sitting in an aluminum webbed chair surveying his surroundings and nursing his diabetic wounds. His avian interests produced many heirs to his passion, and we were promised two hot, wet, baby birds in exchange for a portion of his lot rent. Gary lived on lot number 4, in the pale-blue unit near Tom Seman and next door to Harry's foil-tinted abode.

Right about the time of Darryl Hall & John Oates' "I Can't Go for That," Gary was rubbing his leg wildly complaining of a sore that he wanted my mother to "come take a look at." After summoning my mother, Gary shimmied his Wrangler jeans up his shin to reveal what can best be described as a half-pound of raw hamburger meat crying.

Prior to his weeping wound, Gary had gone on a camping trip wearing his combat boots. The leather had rubbed the front of his shins and caused a bad infection. I'm not sure if he was trying to be a hard-ass or a dumbass, but nature was working against him. Gary had diabetes and, as a result, was unable to win the fight against this recent flesh wound. Six weeks later, he returned from the hospital missing the lower part of his leg—from the knee down. Gary preferred pinning his denim pant leg to the back of his jeans over wearing his prosthetic leg. He was also nice enough to swipe some thirty minibottles of Cepacol mouthwash and alcohol swabs during his stay, and he handed them out to us and the other tenants as gifts.

During the 1980s, there was a big push to get baseball players to chew on gum rather than tobacco, and many convenience stores started shelving pouches of Big League Chew next to pouches of traditional chewing-tobacco brands. Like many of the other tenants, Gary would make frequent beer runs completely inebriated. One immediate result of his bad judgment would result in him grabbing the chewing gum instead of the chewing tobacco. To my knowledge, the only victim of his drunk driving was himself. Angry, he stumbled over to our house and gave my mother his pouches of "Ground Ball" grape-flavored glycerine goodness. To the victor go the spoils.

Steve Winters

Of all the tenants who graced our door, Steve was only one of three who was actually welcome. He had a Napoleonic stature, sported a perfectly coiffed horseshoe mustache, and worked as a truck driver. Steve literally brought his work home, and my little brother was obsessed with his bright-blue rig that was parked on his postage-stamp-sized parking space. Every once in a blue moon, he would be carrying cars on his tractor trailer, which he liked to call *The Grasshopper*. Steve also owned his own mobile home, paid lot rent to my parents, and was apparently a hell-raiser.

I lost count of all the times that my dad had to run out in the middle of the night and bail Steve out of jail after he'd defended the honor of his girlfriend Trisha at The Gold Minor or Godfather's. His rap sheet was filled mostly with assault-and-battery charges and drug possession. Steve's shenanigans never surfaced around me or my siblings. What I remember most about Steve is that he laughed easily, his favorite song was "Bette Davis Eyes" by Kim Carnes, and he was the closest thing we had to family in the park.

Ralph and Vivian

Ralph and his chubby wife, Vivian, lived on lot 5 next door to Florence. Outwardly, Ralph looked as sturdy as John Wayne, but he suffered perpetually from a myriad of pulmonary-related illnesses and had survived two heart attacks, a triple bypass, and countless hospital stays. If you heard an ambulance roar into the park, it was a good bet that it was headed to Ralph and Vivian's lot. Vivian's shameless impertinence was legendary in the park, and when she wasn't scandalmongering, she was preparing high-cholesterol meals for her beloved Ralph.

My mother was convinced that she was trying to off him with her cooking after discovering several pots and pans in their trash cans caked in Crisco and carbon. Ralph was retired, which left him plenty of time to amuse himself by killing lizards, skunks, and harmless black snakes. Ralph's other favorite pastime was chewing tobacco. Unlike Gary, Ralph's drug of choice was saturated fat, and he never was fooled by the marketing tactics of Big League Chew. On one particular afternoon, Ralph offered my six-year-old brother a wad of chewing tobacco. My brother clumsily stuffed a wad in his cheek, immediately threw up on Ralph's shoes, and ran home to tell my mom. To the best of my knowledge, he never touched chewing tobacco again. I made it a point to share this story with Tom Seman later that day, but he already knew about it. Butthole.

David and Donald

On lot 27, next door to Steve Winters, lived two bachelor brothers, David and Donald. I did not know much about them except that they were identical twins. David was clean-shaven, and Donald sported a blond mustache that refused to fully grow in. Their eyes were crystal blue and constantly wild to the point that making eye contact was blinding.

We were threatened within an inch of our lives if we ever went near them or their lot without the presence of my parents or Steve. Apparently, they had repeatedly complained to Tom Seman about being on an FBI watch list for purchasing VHS tapes of young children from Sweden. In spite of Tom's pervy ways, he made it a point to share this with everyone in the park.

Bill Cannidy

Affectionately known as just "Cannidy," he was one of the three tenants who were welcome in our home, and he accompanied us on several local jaunts. You had to love Cannidy. He was always on the lookout for fun, had a contagious laugh, which came easy, and was a walking joke book. His comedic talent was more of a result of overcompensating for his appearance. Cannidy was short, fat, and had early male-pattern baldness. He also liked to come over keyed-up on Jolt Cola and play the Intelevision Skiing game with my dad until the wee hours. His girlfriend and his first wife was named Melinda and had knockers the size of watermelons, which she made a point of showing off in a bikini top, which was as effective as trying to conceal a bowling ball with a Band-Aid.

Cannidy worked in a hospital and often brought home disposable medicine cups used for patients. My mother liked to repurpose the little cups for dispensing the twelve hard-pill vitamins that everyone at the dinner table was required to take each night. She and my grandmother ordered the supplements from a company that they clipped out of the back of a *Reader's*

Digest. She even went through the trouble of trying to be cutesy with the cups by decorating them with wiggle eyes, glue, and a magic marker. Each medicine cup contained:

- Four rose hips Vitamin C 500 mg each
- Two cod liver oil gel caplets (not sure of milligrams)
- Two iron pills (? milligrams)
- One lecithin pill (again, unsure of milligrams, but hey, if it's good enough for Mr. Ed, it's good enough for me)
- Two beta carotene (milligrams varied depending on the level of tan that I was trying to achieve)

Some 70 percent of the time, the purple iron pills caused me to throw up, which may have saved my life from poisoning. The other percentage of the time, I pushed them into the potted plants suspended by rust-colored macramé hangers that my Aunt Laurel had made for my mom. I still keep in contact with Cannidy to this day, and we are able to laugh about the medicine cups, but not the pills.

Bob and Alice

Bob and Alice were the type of couple TV dinners were made for. Alice was an authority on every sitcom that aired between 1962 and 1983. Her favorite was *Diff'rent Strokes*, and she loved to regale me with tales of the Drummonds' latest shenanigans. Bob was the first and one of only two people I have met who has undergone an emergency tracheotomy.

In spite of Bob's best attempts to be understood without his external microphone, issued by the Veteran's hospital and which resembled an electric shaver, we mostly relied on his boneheaded wife, Alice, to translate. His voice resembled the voice coming through the Krystal drive-thru whenever we brought home a sackful of burgers. So my siblings and I decided on the nickname "Drive-thru Bob." Not to his face, of course.

An ex-Green Beret, he was often underestimated due to his lack of a voice, but he was built like a brick shithouse. "Drive-thru Bob" often ridiculed Tom Seman—sometimes to his face—which made him an instant friend of my dad and a trusted ally. "Drive-thru Bob" landed the job of park manager due to his loyalty to my parents and his shared hatred of the tenants.

CHAPTER 4

Government Cheese

AMILY-OWNED-and-operated businesses, no matter what kind, usually meant there were was no enforced age restriction on job roles, hours worked, or pay. It was your duty and responsibility. In order to pocket the most profit from collecting lot rents, the cleaning crew consisted of my mother, myself, and my two siblings—all toiling away at erasing the grime of tenancy.

My older sister Anna's job was mostly to keep a watchful eye on my little brother Jason while he stepped into the world of Joie Chitwood's Thrill Show, complete with a Mr. PiBB cannon jump. In your face, Evel Knievel!

While most kids counted down the days to summer break, I dreaded it. For starters, the heat was oppressive, and, without A/C or a pool, there was little relief outside of the thrill of jumping over the oscillating sprinkler that looked more like a torture device than an irrigation tool. The fun didn't last long, as we had mobile homes to clean, and my father didn't like to waste water. We also risked a sighting from Florence, and you never knew which drunk you would get.

To this day, the traditional scent of Pine-Sol is deeply connected with images of shriveled-up cockroaches on their backs in the traditional death pose and the stench of a Raid fogger. Roaches and palmetto bugs were such a problem in Florida and in our mobile homes that we bought Raid foggers by the gross at the Pace Membership Warehouse. Before I turned six, I could easily tell the difference between a palmetto bug, an American cockroach, and the most dreaded of parasitic insects, the German cockroach. German cockroaches were infinitely smaller, quicker, could lay more eggs, and were much harder to quell from an infestation perspective. However, they did not speak German, but that didn't stop me from fantasizing about them greeting their fellow infestant with a *"Guten Tag."*

Second only to an episode of *Tales From the Crypt*, nothing was scarier or more haunting than an encounter with a flying cockroach—*a.k.a.* a palmetto bug. Sleeping with the windows open was the perfect invitation for an almond-shaped, winged object with soft, feathered wings and hanging black legs to buzz the tower of my and my sister's hair. I grew to recognize the sensation and would wake with flailing arms swinging into the air while retreating to a corner of the room farthest away from the winged bandit.

Anna was able to escape during the day due to school conflicts after returning to Mendenhall Elementary. Jason was still too little to start any program, and my mother decided to send me to a three-day-a-week program at a cinder-block building called the Mickey McGuire Community Center, where I would be exposed to what I had already learned on the street.

Even though it was only a few hours a day, it was a welcome break from cleansing the mobile homes of the sins of its former occupants. It was also a break from my little brother, who was an annoying creature just fifteen months shy of my age.

You could always tell if we parted on good terms with our tenants by the condition of the units and the height of unmowed grass on the lot. If the tenant had been evicted or come close to being kicked out, they might have attempted to flush a perfectly good hairbrush down the toilet. This, of course, led to a flooded bathroom floor. A little known fact—particleboard and water don't mix. This combination could mean that you would literally fall through your ass in the bathroom.

The tenants were also famous for leaving behind not just a mess but really bizarre personal items. Since we didn't rent to tenants with children, there was no chance of say, a Malibu Barbie being left behind. Before we were allowed to enter the mobile home, my mother would first perform a walk-through to shield us from the toxic fogger fumes and random paraphernalia such as a dildo or a dirty syringe. After airing out the mobile home, we were granted entry to ascend the three rusted-out steps and enter the vacated unit.

Empty mobile homes on a hot summer day always had an eery aura about them. The energy of the desperation, happiness, anger, and sadness that went on behind faux, wood-paneled doors seemed trapped in the light and particles that still lingered. Or, it might have been the fumes from the foggers.

On one particular steamy afternoon, I waited to be greenlighted to enter lot number twenty-two. On a small radio, my mother was struggling to fully tune in "Go Your Own Way," by Fleetwood Mac, playing on Q105.

This day, it was different. I stumbled through the front door of lot 22 and into the kitchen. My mother's hands were clumsily clad in bright-yellow cleaning gloves. She was busy cleaning an oven heavily caked in grease drippings. The air was stagnant and filled with the pungent odor of Oven Magic and, of course, fucking Pine-Sol. She was barking orders about staying near her in the unit, but my curiosity called me to the dark hallway. I ignored her and continued down forbidden corridors in just 722 square feet of living space. The air was dancing on the swirling smoke of her Pall Malls.

At the end of the hallway was a stained, double-sized mattress sitting atop a standard box spring, dotted in a Rorschach pattern of brown stains from sweat, bodily fluids, and, perhaps, even excrement.

My goal was to capture the last currency back then that was still immediately spendable by a child—a penny. In fear of touching the many pests that met their fate after the foggers were set off, I was particularly cautious about reaching under the bed.

Tumbling below the rod-iron frame was a nest of dust bunnies and two copper pennies. My hand brushed on a piece of crisp paper. It was a twenty dollar bill. I pocketed the cash instead of turning it over to my parents. To this day, I have not spent it—it remains a symbol of the richest I have felt in my entire life from a monetary standpoint.

That would be my biggest personal score, but, in most cases, the real gold was in the fridge. Most of the tenants were enrolled in government-assistance programs which entitled them to large blocks of gelatinous, processed dairy. Naturally, the cheese was American flavored, and, if it had not been opened and remained untouched, we would bring it home to make sandwiches.

For those of you unfamiliar with what government cheese is, here is the definition according to Wikipedia: *"Government cheese is processed cheese that was provided to welfare and food stamp recipients in the United States from the 1960s through the early 1990s. The style of cheese predated the era, having been used in military kitchens since the Second World War and in schools since as early as the 1960s."*

In 1980, I can tell you that government cheese was supposed to be the flavor of American cheese and came in the shape of a large, rectangular slab, not unlike the orange block of Velveeta that my mother bought for sandwiches. The humiliation of eating this rubbery substance was on par with being caught eating dry dog food. I enjoyed both in absolute secrecy from my peers—even the tenants.

CHAPTER 5

Grandma and Papa

GRANDMA DIDN'T JUST influence my life; she was *The Influencer.* Grandma was tough, fun, and unlike any grandmother I have ever met, and that's what I loved most about her. While other grandmas were concerned over failing knees, ailments, and whether you had enough to eat, Grandma was the first one to grab a raft and head out into the surf, ride in the back of the roller coaster, or take on the steepest water slides. She was also a horrible cook and escaped her place in the kitchen by fixing plates of canned Vienna sausages complete with a side of iceberg lettuce sadly cradling a canned, sliced pear and filled with a dollop of Miracle Whip. If you were still hungry, you usually shut up about it, but if you dared ask for seconds, your plate would be filled with an ice-cream scoop of cottage cheese.

However, Hydrox cookies and Grape Nuts cereal were at your disposal, along with as much sugar as you desired in your tea—cold or hot.

She was also famous for starting the process of pulling down her drawers, her hand down the back of her wedgie-inviting underwear and *on the way* into the entrance of a public restroom would ask in her loudest voice, *"Ang—do you have to go potty?"*

I could really devote an entire book to my Grandma, and that idea is not off the table. She was the master-mind behind my parents' dream of moving to Florida and buying a mobile home park.

She and my mother were very close during my youth, and both of my grandparents were permanent fixtures in my daily life. She owned Placid Lakes Mobile Home Park in Tampa.

Placid Lakes was not like Pelican Mobile Home Park. It was filled with retirees who were either trying to escape children or missing them. Grandma's tenants kept *whole* candy bars to give out to us whenever we came over. No one under the age of fifty-five was allowed to live there during the heyday of the park, and Grandma was the social director.

The recreation hall or "rec hall" had nightly bingo, pinochle, and bridge tournaments. During the summer, one of my siblings or I would get to have a sleepover at my grandparents. I always wanted it to be me, but it was hard to compete with my sister, who was Papa's favorite grandchild. Still, on those nights when Lady Luck was on my side and my sister didn't want to be subjected to the musty smell of old newspapers, cigarette smoke, and canned Harvard beets simmering in the air of the rec hall, I would have the pleasure of collecting candy bars from geriatric fans and turning the bingo cage.

Following the bingo game, Papa would let me lean over his shoulder and peer at his hand during a heated game of pinochle. He was considered one of the most shrewd players, and many wanted to be on his team, including me. In an effort to gain his favoritism, I learned how to trump, when to play a marriage, and what a bare run is.

But it wasn't just hanging out with my Papa or chocolate bars that brought me back to my grandparents' house. They had a crystal-blue, sparkling pool.

We didn't have air conditioning, so spending time there meant surviving the stagnant summer heat.

The pool must have been 75 percent chemicals and 25 percent piss from my "sink or swim" lessons. My grandmother was fun, but she could be tough. By the age of five, I was swimming like Weissmuller from the old *Tarzan* series I used to watch on Nick at Nite.

Still, there were some more tender and generous moments. In addition to swimming lessons, she taught me and Anna how to perfectly apply lipstick by holding our mouth taut and how to keep from blinking while putting on mascara by keeping our eyes wide open in surprise—yes, it works!

Grandma was a single mother in the 1950s and sold Avon products to support my mother and aunt. Based on the amount of sales awards sitting on shelves and curio cabinets, she must have made more than enough to support her daughters without financial support from my biological grandfather, whom I met only a handful of times and who always sent me expensive guilt gifts.

She kept every single miniature white tube of lipstick in shades of tropical coral and red rose and allowed me and my sister to use it liberally, provided we applied it as we were taught.

If my eyes could take the burning from the formaldehyde, I would play dress-up in her closet. Her real fox-fur coats didn't seem to mind the chemicals. I never understood why she just didn't use cedar like other, normal people, but Grandma was not normal.

In spite of her dislike for decorum, she always had a parlor/sitting room and plastic runners over her rugs that left dimpled markings in the carpet—the lasting scars of formality from her troubled youth. It's my contention that people who dress and connect to differing decades are heavily tied to the time in their lives when they felt most alive and connected to themselves.

Like our house at The Pelican Mobile Home Park, Grandma and Papa's house sat surrounded by mobile homes and tenants. It was a white stucco abode that was built in the 1950s, with wooden cabinets that were warped from humidity and use. If you pulled too hard, the magnet might give way, and you would be shot across the room like Bruce Willis in the *Die Hard* movies.

Grandma's living-room entrance was to the immediate right of the front door, and strange strands of very ornate beads hung sadly at random levels and slapped you in the back if you ran through them. Grandma would get angry at us, mostly over the noise produced by our darting through the beads manufactured in Hong Kong.

While my grandparents slept off a night of geriatric debauchery at the rec hall, I got up early on my own, lit the pilot with the motion of one match strike, made hot tea, and raided Papa's stash of Hydrox cookies, stored in the oven that Grandma never used.

Before I could get to the kitchen, I had to crawl across the floor like Rambo thanks to a motion-sensor alarm system installed in Grandma's home in 1983. Unlike our mobile home park that received monthly threats from tenants, Grandma's security system was a preemptive move to protect her and Papa from the crime that was sprouting up in the neighborhood outside of the park.

The red laser beam swept back and forth from the beaded parlor doorway all the way down the hall. You had to time it just right, and as the red light scanned the front door, I shimmied on my belly to the safety of the kitchen table, where I could not be found. A large mirror hanging in the hallway was a valuable tool in my timing.

I can still picture that mirror and easily see my entire childhood flash before my eyes without the need for a near-death experience. Framing my reflection was phony, gold-gilded paint that frequently flaked off. This was the same mirror that I would stare into and wonder what I would look like as an adult or harshly judge my looks.

On a random summer afternoon after swimming in Grandma's pool, I stood in front of that same mirror trying to extract the cracked rubber band that held my long hair in a messy ponytail and stared back at large white blotches all over my dark-tanned forehead, neck, and above my left eye. My reflection looked like someone had poured a bucket of bleach across my forehead, and it ran into my eye and down my neck. My left eyebrow is still stark white; my eyelash has a streak in it, as does my left hairline. At the age of nine, I was diagnosed with a skin condition called "vitiligo," later made famous by Michael Jackson and his real reason for wearing his iconic glove.

I might have dodged some heredity bullets such as a lean figure without exercise, but I experienced a direct hit with this skin condition. Turns out, I was not the milkman's baby, as I was so often accused of due to my differing eye, hair, and lighter skin color from my family. Still, even for a white girl, I tan enough for the lack of pigment to be noticeable and explode across my face.

My dermatologist prescribed a bottle of SPF 15—the highest concentration of sunblock available in 1984. Before that, my parents, like most parents at that time, didn't bother applying sunblock to our scorched backs and shoulders until *after* we showered and showed signs of lobster-red sunburns which later developed into a tan. Today, desperate parents spray and slather their kids with SPF 100, but in the '80s, you didn't wear sunblock until you were already burnt, and even then, it was just SPF 2, maybe a 4—tops.

Kids will be kids, which means that they were total assholes and came up with their own diagnosis of my skin condition—Leprosy. This also explains why even the biggest pop star in the world wore a studded glove and bleached his skin. Due to the fact that I was not black and if I stayed out of the sun long enough I could get my skin color to blend with my Euro-Caucasian ancestors, bleaching was not an option.

However, my mother, being a personal friend of Ra and a regular at causeway beaches, decided it would be easier to have bangs cut into my hair. However, she was sympathetic to my plight and followed doctor's orders to apply the SPF 15 serum to my white spots, but sunblock anywhere else was not deemed necessary.

CHAPTER 6
The Flip Side

Before my ear was open to the first three shuffling chords of Julian Lennon's "Too Late for Goodbyes" on Q105, it was tuned in to that anticipated crackling sound that a needle makes when it first makes contact with a vinyl record.

My parents' album collection is still a very personal and prized possession that is coveted by me for all the right reasons. My exposure to music began *in utero*. My father's obsession with the film *2001: A Space Odyssey* and its soundtrack was one of my first musical memories. I might have been three when I first recognized the haunting and precipitous chords at the beginning of the score.

When my parents first started dating, they sat down and compared their impressive album collections. Out of three hundred albums, they had just four in common. Four months later, they decided to combine their collection and lives and tied the knot in the winter of 1967.

During the years before 1973, when they had their first child and my big sister, Anna, they were able to hear their beloved albums play out in front of them. One lucky night during a live performance of The Paul Butterfield Blues Band in some dirty backroom club in Chicago, Jimi Hendrix showed up and sat in during a jam session.

A short time later (and the term "time" loses its relevance due to the popularity of quaaludes during the '70s) they visited a club to see a singer they had never heard of with a band that they had, Big Brother and the Holding Company. That singer was Janis Joplin and someone my dad described as having a voice that flowed with raw rage and rebellion.

Their sentiment and ear for talent was not lost on their middle child. The album covers and sounds had the same impact on me that my some of my mother's book covers did—fright, insatiable intrigue, and a personality trait that I would later regret.

Music, in particular, was the strongest bond I had with my parents.

The most nightmare-inducing album cover was Queen's *News of the World* album. I couldn't bear to stare back at the empty eyes of a robot that towered the height of a two-story building, carelessly handling the dead bodies of adults—their postmortem stares of terror frozen in time and spilling from his hands the way that dirt-rinsed worms did when I pulled them from their lives in the earth. It made me feel the way that the tenants felt about the currency of life—humans are short-lived and lacked value.

Some of my mother's book covers had the same impact on me. Whenever she left the room, I would flip the paperback cover on its face so that the only thing visible were the many accolades and reviews in favor of the novel.

One disturbing book cover was Ray Bradbury's *The Illustrated Man*. It always reminded me of some of the tenants in the park who offered strange answers after I asked about their teardrop spider and skull tattoos dotted all over their biceps and elbows. My mother later taught me how to spot prison tats and the one telltale sign of those who lacked tattoos but had been incarcerated: they all had read Mickey Spillane's *Mike Hammer* series of books. Incidentally, that was also one of Alice's favorite television shows.

The Beatles, the Moody Blues, Muddy Waters, 10cc, Cat Stevens, and other legends would explode out of hanging speaker boxes painted to look like dice.

Every night before dinner, I found the same connection and bond that they shared with music, and my enthusiasm was rewarded by playing DJ. I followed all the rules of extraction: first I would remove the album from its flimsy paper sheath, and firmly but gingerly holding it *only* by its sides (so that any oils from my fingers wouldn't get on the surface), would perform a one-motion flip that would allow the record to drop gently onto the short pole that jutted out from the center of the turntable.

This might sound easy enough, but one false move, and the mere sound of a record scratch would cross the line between the next song skipping forever and an ass beating—it was the most dangerous thing I did every day, outside of making eye contact with

Florence's glassy gaze as she stumbled home from Godfather's or The Gold Minor.

Any deviation from these exact directions, and my dad would fly into the same level of wrath that me, Anna, or Jason experienced whenever we knocked over a glass of milk and it flowed across the table and spilled directly into his crotch.

After jumping up from the table like lactose was an STD, he would always utter the same phrase: "We can't have anything nice with you kids." Behind the safety of my bedroom door, I would recreate that same scene and line to the delight of Anna and Jason.

My siblings also joined in the dance party in the living room as ELO made our arthritic-jointed Miami Windows tremble. My father was a closeted Electric Light Orchestra fan after seeing the film *Xanadu* at the local drive-in theater. I think he also appreciated Olivia Newton John's ability to "… get physical …" only wearing a leotard that created a camel toe, or crotch cleavage, and a twisted white headband that gathered little to no sweat.

The windows were often open or cracked to suck out cigarette smoke and air so humid you could easily float out of the house—the way that Pepe Le

Pew's feline love interest would be carried away on his scent.

As the landlords of the park, my parents were acutely aware that no one would call the TPD over a noise-ordinance charge—it was one of the few cards of societal defiance they still held in their hands outside of going to work in cut-off jean shorts every day instead of neckties or thermal jumpers.

When noise levels became a nuisance, our park manager, "Drive-thru Bob," would casually stroll over for a quick chat about park happenings. This was a clear decoy to tempering the rattling of our Miami Windows. Thankfully, he rarely dragged Alice away from *The Fall Guy* or repeats of *Hardcastle and McCormick*, so we only had to focus on deciphering his laryngitic sentences.

The hi-def was turned to low, and, when he was done with a debriefing on the latest arrest or Tom Seman's inability to not comment on my mom's breasts, we would set the table for dinner and took advantage of the fact that "Drive-thru Bob" was a polite man who would never accept an impromptu invite to stay for dinner.

CHAPTER 7

Blue Light Special

GRANDMA WAS A permanent fixture at our house, and I don't really remember her walking through the front door—she was just there.

Just before the summer of 1982, Grandma got skin cancer and religion—and not necessarily in that order. At the spry age of fifty-two, Grandma was in no mood for chemo or confession.

After a skin-cancer diagnosis that showed up on the bridge of her nose and freaked her out for reasons related to vanity rather than health, Grandma had taken to wearing my SPF 15 sunblock and a large, floppy white hat that looked like it had been fished out of a dumpster.

The hat paired well with her colorful, striped halter tops and unintentional short-shorts, complete with scalloped piping riding along Grandma's upper thigh and, mercifully, getting trapped in her butt crack. One could argue that Grandma borrowed her style from Florence, but she very seldom imbibed in anything but sweet tea, which she proudly made in the backyard using the power of the sun, wooden clothespins, and three bags of tea.

She half-assed followed and denied her diagnosis by taking copious amounts of Vitamin C tablets purchased from advertisements in the back of the TV *Guide,* which only ignited my mother's desire for all her children to throw back more vitamins from Cannidy's medicine cups at the dinner table.

By the age of six, I was still without any playmates other than my sister and brother because of the park rule about tenants with kids. On the surface, Grandma's tactics might have appeared rugged, but her heart was soft enough to recognize that we were lonely in our new life.

This random summer weekday, she plodded through the office door with Papa—always in her wake—giddy about sharing the news of a woman she had met who waited tables at the local Frisch's Big Boy. Grandma explained that they were both Catholic, although Grandma hadn't stepped foot in a confession booth since Jesus had been a baby. She explained the reason for her excitement.

Her name was Meredith, and, while she was closer to my mom's age, it made perfect sense since Grandma was not like other grandmas and very seldom spent time with women her own age. She seemed to spend most of her time with my mom, and one could argue they might have been best friends. With the exception of the rec-hall events and gatherings, Grandma did not get close to any of the tenants in Placid Lakes Mobile Home Park.

Turns out, Meredith had two daughters who were similar in age and age difference to me and Anna. After fumbling around in her dirty denim purse, Grandma finally fished out a handwritten card. On the cover was a cartoon drawing of a bathing suit and an umbrella. It read: "You are invited to Sarah's 8th birthday party! Join us for cake, chips, and outdoor fun—and don't forget to bring a swimsuit and a towel!"

As a kid, there are few words that strike fear in my heart more than "bring a swimsuit and a towel." I had always been criticized for my inability to metabolize cake at the same rate as Anna and Jason, and I made sure to pack an oversized T-shirt to wear over my electric-green one-piece.

This would be the first birthday party I had been invited to since moving to the park, and, in spite of my resentment at having to participate in a swimsuit, I was beside myself with excitement to the point of nausea.

I quickly plucked the invitation out of Grandma's hands and found a place on our already-crowded refrigerator covered in magnets from places we had never been to. The party was still at least a week away, and I had no idea how I was going to fill my days so that anxiety didn't get the best of me.

Anna and I were already scheming about what to buy her for a birthday present. Should we get her a stuffed Garfield with suction cups for a window in her room, or was she into board games like Mouse Trap?

We normally shopped at Montgomery Ward because it was the department store that carried the largest inventory of items made in noncommunist countries. Which seems strange in today's climate, but I didn't own a pair of plastic anything without Grandma's say. If you wanted a *Where's the Beef?*

nightshirt—and I did—it couldn't be made in The People's Republic of China. However, Hong Kong was okay.

Grandma suggested we pick up something for her little sister, Samantha, who trailed me by just six months in age. Moments later, we all piled into *The Brick* and took off for Kmart.

The local Kmart was crowded, even for a random Tuesday in July. I made a break for the music department. "Abracadabra" by the Steve Miller Band was rudely interrupted by a large flashing blue light—the kind that Roscoe P. Coltrane flashed when he was in hot pursuit of the Duke boys.

Grandma followed the light and the booming sound of a man using a miniature bullhorn advertising jelly or "jellies" shoes for only $4.99! Anna and I had longed for a pair of these brightly colored blister-makers that we planned on wearing with socks on special occasions and without socks for a more casual look.

Grandma, being Grandma, immediately checked the label to make sure it was not manufactured in a communist country. In raised gelatin letters were the words "Made in China." My heart sank, and, in a consumerist moment, I sat in silent protest and cradled a pair of pink jellies in my arms. At this point, my sobbing began attracting more attention from fellow shoppers than the turning blue bulbs.

My display of despair was not tolerated by Grandma, and she uttered the line I had always dreaded: "Whoever told you that life was fair?"

After my temper tantrum, Anna and Jason took turns imitating my performance, and I took turns throwing missed punches as they took advantage of my emotions and dodged every flailing punch.

After much discussion, we all made a unanimous decision that Sarah would really enjoy the game Sorry, and, for Samantha, we picked out a Princess Power Paper Doll book. This gave me hope that I would have something in common with Samantha since I had a pretty impressive Holly Hobbie paper doll collection.

A week later, Grandma showed up to take us to Sarah's soiree and brought along a pair of pink jellies for me and purple ones for Anna. At some point she had slipped over to Monkey Ward's (her nickname for Montgomery Ward) a week earlier and kept them until Sarah's birthday party.

I knew Grandma's heart well enough to realize that, while she didn't wear it on her sleeve, she kept it tucked away, even when I later threw my arms around her in my most generous gesture of thanks.

CHAPTER 8
Slip 'n' Slide

SARAH AND SAMANTHA'S house sat in an established neighborhood that was a mixture of well-kept ranch-style homes and dilapidated bungalows with dirt yards and rusty chain-link fences.

On the post of a sagging section of chain link, a shriveled pink balloon hung on for dear life. Sarah and Samantha's house was one of those dirt-yard bungalows. It never occurred me that you could be poor and not live in a mobile home.

I'll never forget the excitement on Sarah's face as she bounded out the front door and across the severely damaged pathway thriving with tall weeds popping through the cracked concrete. Apparently, Grandma had been spending quite a bit of time at their house over the last few months, and Sarah leaned into Grandma's felt-piped shorts for a hug.

We were a bit early, and I was relieved that Anna and I didn't have to drag Jason to the party. Nevertheless, my mother fought hard for his attendance, as most mothers do when they want to get every kid out of the house for some much-needed time to themselves.

Anna did the honors and thrusted Sarah's birthday present, wrapped in the Sunday comics, toward her. Sarah appreciatively accepted the gift and walked us through the maze of weeds. Anna and I immediately took a liking to Sarah—she was genuine and shared our optimism for friendship.

I still had Samantha's gift clutched in my hand and was anxious to see her reaction to it—also, the funny-papers ink had begun to stain the palms of my hands. Before I could climb the three, steep, concrete steps leading to the front door, I was knocked on my ass by a lively border collie named "Duchess."

Grandma was hissing at Duchess to calm down, but Duchess sensed my acceptance of being trapped on my back and took the opportunity to get in some sloppy licks of affection.

Their house had clearly been tidied to the best of Meredith's ability, which was similar to my mother's level of cleanliness. Let's just say God wouldn't be pleased. On a transistor radio, Meredith was fumbling with the rabbit ears to tune in an easy-listening station. Just when she was about to give up and began hollering for Sarah and Samantha's dad to step in, Spyro Gyra's "Morning Dance" boomed through the tinny speakers.

Samantha followed her mom out of the bathroom, clearly traumatized by the pain and patience required to remove the rat nest of tangles that had long been neglected. Sarah was smart and, like me, had a pixie cut and—also like me—hers was for deeper, more emotional reasons outside of hygiene or beauty maintenance.

I shyly handed over my gift with the predisposed notion that she would immediately cheer up after being scalped with a steel-toothed hairbrush by her mother. Samantha carefully began unwrapping her present until she got a glimpse at She-Ra's recognizable crown, and the funnies fell to the floor.

In one motion she grabbed my arm and pulled me into her and Sarah's bedroom to show off her Fashion Plates creations stuck to the wall with yellowed scotch tape. Sarah and Anna quickly joined us and, we sat in a semicircle surrounding their Barbies discussing our favorite cartoons, toys, and the pain of hair brushing.

We were so wrapped up in our immediate connection and friendship that we almost forgot Sarah had a birthday party to host.

Mike—or "Mr. O'Connell"—rapped gently on the door, and when we didn't answer barged through the room playfully growling like a large grizzly bear and threatened to eat off all our feet if we didn't comply with his demands that we come outside to check out the outdoor water activities he had set up for the party.

On the south side of the lawn was *the* Slip 'n' Slide I had seen advertised endlessly every Saturday morning between *The Smurfs* and Warner Bros. cartoons. Over the long, yellow tarp-like strip was a stream of mud-infused water coming from a sprinkler hose that had seen better days.

I met Sarah's eyes and immediately shared her unspoken apprehension to donning a swimsuit—never mind the exhilaration of speeding across a mixture of the last remaining shreds of grass, mud, and flinty-scented fluids pumping through a garden hose.

Mr. O' Connell, a big kid himself, passed over his can of Stroh's beer to Sarah to hold and, walking about ten feet behind the grounded slide, gained speed from a running start and launched himself into an out-of-control skid that carried him beyond the landing pad, only to be stopped by a Radio Flyer wagon.

This is the kind of behavior I had never witnessed from my father but always wished I had. We all ran over to him out of genuine concern only to find him in a fit of hysterical laughter. His heaving guffaws had torn Grandma and Mrs. O' Connell from their intense discussion in the kitchen. Grandma ran over to the scene and gave Mr. O' Connell a more-comedic-than serious tongue lashing while wagging her lit Pall Mall in his face. He took it in stride and, brushing himself off, stood up, cracked a fresh beer, and got ready for more guests.

Duchess was not far behind the chaos and was loving every minute of it, including a good cooling off on her warm fur from the water hose.

The party was a relatively small affair with a total of fewer than ten kids—mostly girls and one token boy from Sarah's class. Meredith and Grandma had retreated to the kitchen to dump out the butts from bean-bag-bottomed ashtrays and to empty bags of potato chips into plastic bowls.

Meredith popped back out to lead the party-goers to the house's cramped bedrooms and the only bathroom to change into our swimsuits, where I got a better look at their eclectic decor. It seemed to have quite a bit in common with my own home. Apparently, both her and my parents had attached the memories from the best years of their lives to their interior-decorating style. Or perhaps, they couldn't bear to part with items that they had grown attached to or had simply stopped noticing even if they had become an eyesore.

Sarah's living room had two lumpy antique sofas, a coffee table with seahorses in the glass that was heavily lacquered, and, in the corner, a shrine to Hulk Hogan, complete with posable action figures, posters, and a red Hulkamania headband. A giant Miller Lite piggy bank filled with pennies doubled as a door stop in the master bedroom. On the floor, a mattress lay directly on the floor, surrounded by tumbleweeds of Duchess's fur.

We had the same piggy bank in our home and the same kind of odd theme. In a corner of our living room was a hanging ashtray, a rusty boom lamp, mushroom ottoman, those dicey speaker boxes, and an antique oil painting of George Washington. I've been told that these items are alive and well today—the mushroom ottoman has been restored to its former glory, and the boom lamp is still operational.

Meredith was quite proud of her collection and noticed me looking curiously at the seahorses trapped in the coffee table. She explained that it was a gift from Mike on their anniversary, because seahorses mate for life. I was struck by how much this gift meant to her and hoped that I would marry someone that would be my seahorse.

The party went off without a hitch and ended with me slamming—not sliding—on the water activity outside—knocking the wind of out me to the point that I had trouble finding space in my lungs to suck in air. Grandma responded by reminding me that life wasn't fair and uttering my second-most-hated statement about life, "Suck it up, buttercup."

Playdates didn't exist back then, so our next meet-up was casually scheduled for some day next week, and Sarah and Samantha were to be dropped off at our mobile home park for some playtime.

I felt a stronger bond with Sarah—even though she was the older of the sisters—for many reasons, beginning with how our mothers regarded our weight and body shape and an awareness that we were both embarrassed of our lower societal class of life.

CHAPTER 9

I Want My Color TV

ON THE CORNER OF our Formica kitchen counter, and next to our touch-tone beige phone that we used to call time, was the most-watched and one of two televisions in my whole house. The eleven-inch Zenith had two dials and a set of long antennas that were affectionately nicknamed "rabbit ears" (the cute name helped to curb frustration when a channel signal failed to transmit clearly) and transmitted only in black-and-white.

Similar to the first person who attempts to open a jar of pickles, adjusting the rabbit ears had the same effect. Someone else always believed that they had the magic touch and could make it flicker to life and bring in a better image. Grandma's nickname for any television was "the boob tube," but I liked Papa's nickname better—"the idiot box"—and they used it freely whenever they couldn't get the channel in, either.

The dinner table was relatively quiet and without distraction until my parents discovered Judge Wapner and the cast of characters on *The People's Court*. Their connection to the show, I believe, had much to do with the time that they had spent in a courtroom or courthouse going through the motions of evictions. As I mentioned in the Mobile Home Park Owners glossary, evictions took several months, time, and emotions and could quickly turn dangerous. It was a welcome sound to hear my parents sporadically break into uncontrollable laughter after always seeing them stressed about dealings with the tenants.

The show would open with the same line—"What you are about to witness is real. The participants are not actors. They are the actual people who have already either filed suit or been served a summons to appear in a California (or New York Metropolitan) Municipal Court. Both parties in the suit have agreed to dismiss their court cases and have their disputes settled here, in our forum."

Following the intro opening, Judge Wapner would address the court with the same line at the beginning of each episode: "I know you've all been sworn, and I have read your complaint," and we would be poised to hear him dispense his verdict and polite insults directed at the intellectually challenged. I picked up on the fact that if you showed up to Wapner's courtroom, you should always bring a notarized affidavit by anyone who sticks up for you but couldn't be there.

Our favorite episodes always featured neighbors and dog bites. The plaintiffs and defendants would often show up to court with their pooch as a testament to its temperament, but that usually backfired, and sometimes the dogs would even attack the show's commentator, Doug Llewelyn, during a postverdict interview.

The small, shitty television might have been for dinnertime watching, but on Saturday mornings, it belonged to me and my siblings. Thankfully, my parents tended to sleep beyond 9:00 a.m. and even later if Cannidy or Steve and Trisha came over to play Burger Time or Revenge of the Beefsteak Tomatoes.

I was an early riser, but sometimes my brother would beat me to the punch because whoever got up the earliest controlled what cartoon was on. Plus,

I could dump mounds of sugar on my unsweetened puffed wheat cereal without judgment from my mom.

The Smurfs always seemed to be on, but, in reality, they most likely ran on and off all morning up until Dr. Paul Bearer introduced a horror film on the show *Creature Feature* with his ghoulish cohost Elvira, Mistress of the Dark.

Everything was usually copasetic until a scheduling conflict occurred between the air times of *G.I. Joe: A Real American Hero* and *Shirt Tales*. The fighting would escalate into fists, and the noise would wake up my sister, who would then proceed to beat the shit out of me and my brother followed by a slew of slurs such as, *butthole, Der-bag,* or just *butthead*. Still, this would restore temporary peace among the three of us, and my sister, being the oldest, would break the tie on what we would watch—which usually meant Bugs Bunny, Peppy Le Pew, or Hanna Barbera's *Hair Bear Bunch*.

Under no circumstances were we to go near the thirty-two-inch Zenith television in the living room. For one, the living room was right outside of my parents' bedroom. They could probably sleep through the fistfights but not the sound of cartoons. Second, we had just bought our first, brand-new VCR, and we were reminded on a daily basis that it cost more than $1,000. My parents were quite familiar with the inner workings of a cassette recorder, as video cassettes had the same guts and moving parts as a reel-to-reel audio tape player.

One thing that we could agree on watching was *The A-Team, The Dukes of Hazzard, Knight Rider,* or even *The Fall Guy.* On some occasions, we even shared our TV with Papa because he was the only adult who wanted to watch *Hardcastle and McCormick.* My parents and Grandma hung out after coming over for a dinner of overcooked pork chops and applesauce.

There were some pluses to being a mobile home park owner. For instance, CATV, or cable television, was not available in every household. By 1984, the Cable Act created a sort of boomtown for television channels. However, it was still hard to get and expensive, so my parents bargained with the cable company—they would allow our park to be wired for cable so that tenants like Alice could ramp up her couch-potato time, and, in exchange, we would get cable at our house for free.

Our package included every movie channel, including Disney, HBO, Nickelodeon, Cinemax, and the most dreaded of channels for every parent at the time, MTV. Nickelodeon became a fast favorite of mine because of the show *You Can't Do That on Television*—I always wanted to get slimed. And the Disney channel didn't air *Snow White, Pinocchio,* or *Cinderella*—those films were released only in theaters. Instead, you got the best of Disney's strange side.

The Disney franchise was quite taken with Don Knotts and Tim Conway's synergy and showed family favorites like *The Apple Dumpling Gang* and *The Apple Dumpling Gang Strikes Again* (I didn't care for the sequel). Every once in a while, Disney has to go back to the dark side of storytelling with real-action films like *The Black Hole*, which was about the theory that black holes in space were actually the portal to hell. Sweet dreams, kids. Or, *Escape to Witch Mountain*, where the old guy from *Green Acres* helps these two kids with weird psychic powers escape in his Winnebago from a rich guy who wants to kidnap them.

Kidnapping plots were a constant theme in almost every television series or movie when I was a kid, and yet these two characters went ahead and trusted an old guy camping alone in a Winnebago. Then again, they were psychic, so it all worked out.

It was confusing that the kidnapping storyline that was threaded into almost everything that we watched did not seem to faze my mother, but if MTV came on, my mother's head would explode, which, in hindsight, would have made for a great music video.

She became fond of quoting Bill Cosby whenever she complained to other moms and my grandma about MTV—"It's nightmares set to music."

One bonding moment with my brother was the day that he discovered our mother's technological ineptitude. All cable channels in the early '80s were analog, and the cable box had to be set on top of your television. You could stream channels by turning the dial to 02 or 04. My mother was never aware of this fact and believed that she had blocked MTV and anything else inappropriate channeled through 02.

We wanted our MTV, and we would not be denied VH1.

To date, I can honestly say that I have never had a nightmare from watching any of my favorite music videos from the '80s. However, I still have the occasional nightmare about being kidnapped for my psychic propensities by Eddie Albert in a motorhome.

CHAPTER 10

Matterhorns and Milk

HAD LONGED TO START school the year before, but, as stated earlier, my mother wanted me to be at home with her a little longer. Her reasoning was that the government was trying to snatch children *too early* from the bosom of mothers. Or perhaps, she needed me to clean mobile homes. Either way, I blame her subscription to *The Phyllis Schlafly Letter*. Phyllis's black-and-white head-shot and beehive hairdo often stared back at me from its resting perch on top of the mustard-colored, furry bathroom scale next to the toilet.

I did take pride in my toilet-scrubbing skills and from an early age exhibited a penchant for organization and cleanliness, but a social life outside of the park took priority. In fact, you could walk into the bedroom that I shared with my sister and note early signs of OCD when you compared my side of the room with Anna's, decorated in plump piles of dirty T-shirts and grass-stained jeans.

Skinny, funny, and full of life, Anna's dark brown hair matched her chocolate-colored eyes. In fact, along with my brother Jason, there was no mistaking that they shared the same parents. She was drastically different from me in many ways, including the fact that I had blond hair and blue eyes and could not eat whatever I wanted. Because my inherited physical looks differed drastically from my family, I was frequently called "the milkman's baby" by tenants and total fucking strangers who may or may not have realized that they were calling me a bastard and accusing my mother of having a love child.

As the oldest sibling, everything Anna did or owned was superior to mine, including my most cherished possession at that time, a Pink & Pretty Barbie. I worshipped Anna and was thrilled to have an official third-grader accompany me to my kinder- garten classroom.

My first day of school at Mendenhall Elementary was one of the most anticipated and exhilarating moments of my early life. I will never forget my outfit that day—a brown-striped turquoise turtleneck sweater dress that looked like it was straight out of a *Brady Bunch* yard sale. I hated turtlenecks and fought my mother all morning over my *chosen* outfit choice—a pair of high-water cords and a yellow Dukes of Hazzard iron-on photo T-shirt of the General Lee flying over Roscoe P. Coltrane's police car. Plus, my name was ironed on across the back of the shirt although I had to trash it after too many washes and the glue gave way, leaving only the letters, GIE.

Walking into the classroom, I was captivated by the amount of arts and crafts hanging on strings of colorful yarn and cut-outs of tiny hands with the names of students proudly displayed.

After admiring these handwoven masterpieces, I was led to a large Formica table and to where I would be sitting. A handwritten note displaying my name was facing my chair, and I eagerly took my seat. After a quick meet-and-greet with the teacher and other students, I was strangely aware that I was socially awkward and had no idea how to act around my peers or anyone under the age of forty-five who didn't spend their days watching soap operas, puffing on Camels, and sipping on a Hamm's beer.

Sitting Indian style in a circle, we spent our morning meeting inflatable characters called "The Letter People," with strange cartoonish teeth that were passed around while we practiced phonics. We also worked at memorizing our phone number and home address.

I was a bit bored because my mother had gone through considerable trouble to teach me to read, but the social aspect was so significant to me, and my life was forever changed that day after being introduced to Mellow Smellow Scratch 'n' Sniff stickers. No longer would I be denied the pizza and popcorn my siblings could have because of my sluggish metabolism, which I'd inherited along with my hair and eye color. I could now have my cake and eat it, too, even if it was inhaled through my nose instead of my mouth.

Another thrill and a close second to stickers infused with chemicals and scents that made you want to eat was access to cartons of chocolate milk purchased for thirty-five-cents. I turned in my sweaty coins, clutched in my small fist to my kindergarten teacher, Mrs. Bastley, and was handed a popsicle stick with the letter "C" on it. Those who wanted to drink white milk were clearly never exposed to my diet and were handed a "W" popsicle stick.

Our snacks-of-the-day were handed over as well, and, knowing that mine would be either celery sticks or a freckled banana, I didn't bother getting excited over the contents of the paper bag.

Following Mrs. Bastley's instructions to walk single file from the classroom door to the cafeteria door, I took the security of this popsicle stick seriously, and, clutching the cheap, pressed wood in my left hand and flimsily holding the paper snack bag in my right hand, I walked nervously and stoically through the propped-open door toward the maddening sound of child chatter echoing in the cafeteria while clad in my turquoise nightmare.

While my classmates busted out Kudos snack bars and Sunkist Fruit Snacks, I opened my snack to reveal a mashed-to-hell banana. Adding insult to injury, I managed to screw up opening the carton of chocolate milk by not pushing in the cardboard and pulling it out by the sides. Instead, I tore it across the section and shredded what should have been a spout. Desperate to get the chocolaty goodness to my lips, the milk ended up running down my turquoise torment dress and found a home in the tightly blended wool fibers, further souring my day and that godawful dress.

When you really hate what you are wearing, the only thing that can make it worse besides smelling like sour milk is any attention being brought to you in that cloak of shame. It doesn't necessarily have to be a bully. It could be something trivial, like being chosen from an audience of several hundred kids in an elementary cafeteria in front of the whole school to hold up the end of a Matterhorn while grown men from the local German Club clumsily perform like Clark W. Griswold in lederhosen.

On the car ride home, my mother tried extracting details from me and my sister, making sure to focus on my day since school was a relatively new concept to me. As a parent, she went to the usual line of questioning whenever any kid returned from a day of learning. Did you learn anything new? Did you make new friends? Did you have a good day? All of the aforementioned lines of questioning were all easily squashed in any American household with just three words: "Good," "yeah," or "fine."

Pulling into our recently paved driveway, I saw Gary perfectly perched on his stoop and waving from the seat of his rainbow-webbed lawn chair. He seemed more worked up today than that time I told him I loved Ronald Reagan and he chased me off his porch with a full can of beer sloshing in one hand and a crutch in the other.

This time, I quickly studied his face and realized that he was excited about his pet cockatiels, Ralph and Trixie.

CHAPTER 11

Baby Birds

AFTER GARY HAD LOST his left leg to stupidity and diabetes, he convinced my mother that he needed the birds to lift his spirits. Just like allowing the cable company inside the park, my mother allowed Gary's birds only if she was going to get covered in the end. Gary was convinced he could make some dough selling baby birds, but this being his first stab at his new venture, he offered up two of the five eggs that Trixie had laid to us—they would be our very first family pets.

This was just the kind of distraction that I needed to forget the Matterhorn, turquoise, and soured milk. I dropped my book bag and bolted out of *The Brick* before my mother could stop me. For the past three weeks and under the watchful eye of my parents, I had daily check-ins on the aviary nursery—which was basically a heating pad/fire hazard under Gary's sleeper sofa.

I followed the direction of Gary's exuberant voice and his crutch. Perched on a small bed consisting of moist towels worn from bleach and use, sat two of the ugliest and most vulnerable creatures that I had ever seen—I was in love.

For the first time in my life, I had seen the look of unconditional love in my mother's eyes and an un-triggered, instinctual reaction rather than the forced, conjured feelings of motherhood that I had felt from her.

Their eyes were still closed, and my mother personally hand-fed them 'round the clock. In an era where there was no Internet, she had done her homework on how full their crops should be and the fact that they would imprint on her when their eyes finally opened. She named them "Marcus" and "Quintus" after the Ciceronian brothers who helped shape politics in ancient Rome.

When you're a child, you always think your parents are the smartest and most educated people walking the earth. Truth be told, this was the first indication to me that my mother possessed an above-average IQ.

That and she was *always* reading a book—never romance novels but authors like Ayn Rand, Ray Bradbury, and Ken Follett. These books also influenced my reading list as I grew older. At first, I read them mostly to please her and get the attention which I yearned for during my childhood and beyond.

However, she also used books as an excuse to not only escape life but having to be entirely present and engaged with her children, which I believed was not entirely her fault—she must have been bored to tears watching *Schoolhouse Rock* and sounding out vowels.

While she wasn't vain and very seldom wore makeup or dresses, she understood that she was blessed with a trim figure and natural beauty that required little enhancement.

My mother's nurturing and care of Marcus and Quintus was on par with the skill level and attention of a zoologist. One of our favorite theme parks, Busch Gardens, had a bird show featuring colorful macaws that would fly to their trainers when commanded. Even more impressive, they had learned to roller skate.

My siblings and I decided the first trick our pet birds should learn was roller skating. We went to work on our own little chop shop removing the tires from my brother's least favorite Hot Wheels cars and the plastic seat belts from my Barbie DreamVette because we didn't use seat belts in real life, and why should Barbie?

Marcus and Quintus were very gentle creatures and never pecked or bit any of us *until* we tried getting them to curl their talons to a popsicle stick, Hot Wheels tires, and repurposed Barbie seat belts.

While the roller-skating training was considered a big fail, they did learn to fly to us when we called their names. Quintus was the most impressive and learned to whistle "Bridge on the River Kwai." He was also drawn to anything that matched his bright-yellow crest, including my dad's bottle of Nuprin, which my dad popped like candy on a daily basis.

Sadly, we didn't have Marcus very long. My dad found him at the bottom of the cage one morning. It was the first time I saw my dad get sad over anything. My mother retreated to her books, and I followed her lead.

Quintus went on to live a long and full life until fifteen years later, when he flew off my mother's shoulder, out the back door, and—like most of the tenants who left the park—was never to be seen or heard from again.

CHAPTER 12

Hammies

GROWING UP, I always wanted a dog of our own. That's why my mother got us hamsters. Rats, mice, or any small, furry animal with a tail longer than a grain of rice were out of the question, because their lives would be threatened by the Raid foggers we used to extinguish roaches if they ever escaped from their orange, plastic containers—tubes leading to nowhere.

Following the sudden and devastating loss of Marcus, my siblings and I finally pled our case that we needed a rodent to soften the blow of death. Near Grandma's Kmart was Petland—my favorite place to safely view nurse sharks and tarantulas, and window shop for pets. But no amount of petitioning would ever sway my parents to allow a puppy or kitten.

Our first pet hamster—and, oddly enough, the only one to die of natural causes—was named "Moses."

Moses was our most beloved hamster and had pretty brown-and-white markings, but the only living being in our house that was not as enchanted with Moses was our only surviving cockatiel, Quintus, who seemed ever confused about his standing in nature and laid low behind his own safe space of bars.

For two years, Moses very seldom bit us, no matter how many times he was smothered by small, sweaty hands 'round the clock. A little more than two years later, Moses was enjoying his golden years when he was struck down with what the vet called a stroke. His funeral was heartbreaking for me and my siblings.

I can still picture his "coffin"—an old shoebox from a pair of beloved Florsheim's that my dad never wore except to my dance recitals or school plays.

In our grief, my mother took us to Petland for our next victim. It was my turn to pick, and I chose a white, fluffy, red-eyed albino hamster aptly named "Popcorn."

I loved Popcorn, but my affections were not returned. Popcorn's new habitat had once been a birdcage and had been procured while on a trip to the dump—technically, the "transfer station"—with my Papa, followed by breakfast at his favorite greasy spoon, Hog Heaven.

My mom helped me wash off the old filth and caked-on bird poop, and we presented Popcorn with his new surroundings. He didn't take well to it. Each night, true to his albino roots, he would climb to the top of his cage and drop about three feet to the bottom—the equivalent of jumping out of your second-story window.

This would continue 'round the clock and into the wee hours of the morning, and Anna and I had to learn to sleep through the noise, which was less comforting than what we had become accustomed to—sweltering temperatures and police radios.

It was later explained to me that albino animals tend to go insane. This information would have been helpful at the time of our purchase. He also was the most aggressive, and he bit the shit out of me on several occasions.

I had to quit telling my mom about his attacks to avoid being dragged to the family MD for yet another tetanus shot.

I decided to leave the madness and the sound of a hamster dropping on its back all night and headed over to Sarah and Samantha's house for a sleepover. Following a night of prank calls goading random people about cats in their gardens and fridges running away, I returned home to a warm hug from my mom. My stomach dropped, and I knew what had happened. She had found Popcorn in between the bars of his cage in his final attempt to free himself from the confines of his human captors.

My next pet, Muffin, was a gentle soul with long, fluffy hair and unique markings. In his desperation to be free, he ate away at the bottom of his cage and ingested metal shavings, which caused him to bloat to the size of a water balloon. After we gave him Tums and Altoids, he succumbed to his fate the following morning.

Perhaps the most heartbreaking of those stories was the tale of Sniffles.

Sniffles met his fate one unbearably hot Florida afternoon in the summer of '83. We had decided to go sightseeing for the day, and upon my grandmother's assurance that he would be OK, we left him on the front seat of our '81 Chevy pickup. We returned from a day of sightseeing, and I found Sniffles literally "fried" to the bottom of the cage like a tater tot.

I could tell that Grandma felt bad, but, being Grandma, she repeated her favorite phrase, "Whoever told you life was fair?" Grandma's blasé approach to Sniffles' death stemmed from how she and her generation emotionally survived The Great Depression and World War II.

CHAPTER 13

Doobies at Disney

IN SPITE OF LIVING IN a mobile home park, we still dropped the cash to visit theme parks. We lived only an hour away from Disney World, and Busch Gardens was down the street. We had seasonal passes to the Disney parks before annual passes existed. We were annual pass holders to the Tampa theme park Busch Gardens and seasonal pass holders to its water park, Adventure Island.

Adventure Island is a labyrinth of faux rock formations with winding tubes and slithering cement slides. Tons of sand had been brought in to create minibeaches, but the sand would often get too hot to walk on for more than five seconds. Outside, food was allowed, so Grandma made sure that we packed a cooler full of freezer-bread sandwiches. Grandma would buy four loaves of day-old bread and store them in the freezer. The bread never got the chance that it needed to fully thaw, so the bologna would take on the taste of freezer burn and Miracle Whip. Missing from the contents of the Playmate cooler was my mom's beer.

In a red-and-white Coleman jug, we all took turns swigging moldy lemonade from the Wyler's mix made with just half the suggested sugar on the packet. By the time you worked up the courage to take a swig from the jug, you were rewarded with the puckering flavor, dehydration be damned.

While my siblings and I lunched on freezer-bread sandwiches and moldy lemonade, we sat across from the snack bar, where water-park patrons stood in line for two-decker Tampa sandwiches—towering with stacks of assorted meats and cheeses and four-layer slices of chocolate cake. Adding to the rancid taste of our meal, the snack bar was at least eight feet higher than our lunching pad, so the patrons could look down on the serfs chewing their day's allowance.

One hot summer afternoon, inspired by Genesis's "Throwing It All Away" playing on piped-in speakers throughout the park, I did the unthinkable. Under the cover of a beach towel and a chaise lounge, I waited for a family to abandon their feast and stole the leftovers for myself—gobbling them up as fast as I could outside of a public restroom. To this day, I struggle more with the shame of not including my brother and sister in my heist over the fact that I ate food left behind by strangers outside of a public restroom in my bare feet and wearing a lime-green bathing suit.

Following the secret success of my mission, Grandma wanted us all to put our swimming lessons to the test in the wave pool. The wave pools of the early '80s were not the wave pools of today. They were typically ten feet or deeper, rafts or floats in all shapes and sizes were welcome, and the waves were endless.

Of course, we would carry out our dare of swimming to the deep end when the waves really got going. On one memorable occasion, I had to punch another kid in the nose after he grabbed my little brother's head and began pulling him under, causing him to panic. Grandma was proud of me because she had taught me that same move. Little-known lifeguarding fact: you can subdue panicked victims by pulling their hair.

Disney World turned out to be the happiest place on earth for me and my siblings—as did its answer to a water park, River Country. It was the only place that Grandma was on her best behavior outside of the potty routine and the one day at a theme park that was not met with a hair shirt and a Coleman cooler.

It seemed to have the opposite effect on my mother. She regarded Disney World with the same contempt she had for the decorum and societal manners of growing up in the suburbs of the 1950s.

The one time we went to Disney World without Grandma and Papa, Steve Winters and Trisha came along. My mother, who detested thrill rides, insisted that Anna, Jason, and I ride on the WEDWay People Mover in Tomorrowland with them until Steve and Trisha finished smoking a doobie in one of the moving transports away from us.

Grandma got wind of the said incident and vowed never to miss another visit to the park. True to her word and true to form, she took me, Anna, and Jason on Space Mountain, Thunder Mountain Railroad, and her favorite, The Carousel of Progress, which rewarded her with some much-needed nostalgia. Grandma had already been on this ride at the 1964 New York World's Fair with her second husband, whom I never met.

It was the one ride we all agreed upon. Papa would often fall asleep for one of his afternoon naps that occurred so often that we feared he had narcolepsy. I loved it for its theme song titled, "The Best Time of Your Life."

My mother loved "The Best Time of Your Life" song so much that, when she learned that the attraction would be changed to its original song, "There's a Great Big Beautiful Tomorrow," she snuck in my Sony Walkman in her purse—aptly nicknamed "Mammoth Cave"—and recorded the tune while the ride was going so she could transcribe it.

As for the WEDWay People Mover, it's still a real hoot if you've got sciatica, a heart condition, narcolepsy, or if you want to get stoned and people-watch. Disney has since upped its game and you can scarcely hide smoking a cigarette, let alone a joint.

I'm often asked why I am so obsessed with Disney, and my answer is not the princesses, the costumed characters, manufactured magic, or the contact high. It was the one place that my family behaved (when Grandma was around) and the one place I was able to feel a part of the world that I was so often and deeply divided from at school and outside of the park.

CHAPTER 14

Career Day

AS ENTREPRENEURS, my parents were work brickle. They reported for duty much earlier than most other people, wore cut-off jeans and T-shirts, and answered to nobody wearing a tie. This suited them well.

In school, my fellow classmates were mostly white families who had the means to afford to pay for a better life. Their kids carried Trapper Keepers with bright palm trees or a shiny red Lamborghini on the cover and further bragged about it by having the nerve to pull the cover open and release that sound that only Velcro can make when it's separated from cloth. Their signs of wealth extended to their lunchboxes, which contained refreshing Capri-Sun pouches and Ho-Hos.

These parents wore suits and went to an office each day breathing artificial air and wearing the uniforms of outward success. Their kids wore faces of pride when their parents came to school on Career Day and discussed their daily adventures of soaring through the skies on 747s for Pan Am or designing the cereal box for Smurf Berry Crunch—which, due to my diet, I was never allowed to eat as a part of my balanced breakfast.

Sarah and Samantha also lived the same confusing dichotomy of a double life. They ended up attending private Catholic schools and were at constant odds with their station in life, not shared with those around them in our scholastic worlds.

Our parents fished hairbrushes out of toilets, slung hash, and worked various blue-collar jobs. We didn't live in large sprawling suburbs like Tampa's Carrollwood community, where sagging chain-link fences were prohibited by HOAs.

Sarah and Samantha's parents reacted by pushing their daughters over the divide in their studies and sports so they could attend college on a scholarship.

My mother reacted by insisting that college was not necessary to elevate our station in life or provide us a better future. After all, we wouldn't need it because of our private-school education.

In reality, my mother's vanity was strongly tied to her intellect, and that meant that we were worthy adversaries in her daily intellectual banter. But a college degree could mean a fair advantage above her education level. The threat was too great, and she often coped with my ideas of higher education with alcohol-induced tantrums.

Sleepovers with classmates were always a challenge for me and Anna, so most sleepovers happened with Sarah and Samantha. We had a bond, an understanding. We were so embarrassed about where we lived that we felt comfortable only around each other.

CHAPTER 15

Causeway Beaches

THE ONLY THING THAT I fucking hated more than cleaning the units during the summer was going to the beach with my mom. It wasn't just about sweating wearing a swimsuit—which my mother used as an excuse to foist a new celery-vegetable soup diet on me—it was really just about sweating.

I remember the first time I learned about tapeworms while watching *Ripley's Believe It or Not* with Papa. Jack Palance's sultry cowboy voice would introduce the image of an intestinal tapeworm devouring everything in its victim's stomach before they got a chance to digest it.

I had to ask Grandma twice if this was real, and she confirmed that it was and continued to walk down the hallway, gagging past the mirror where I'd discovered the skin condition that I had in common with Michael Jackson. All the while, Grandma would try to tempt me away from the TV to play a game of Scrabble.

But the only thing that could drag me away from a triple letter and word count on a "z" was the most important piece of television I had seen since Baby Jessica was rescued from a well. With a tapeworm, maybe I could eat what my family did without the ignominy, the calories, or the weight gain.

After this amazing educational show, I hatched a plan to catch a tapeworm. One late afternoon, my dad caught me sticking my finger into and licking the soy sauce that floated on the top of the uncooked pork chops that he intended to turn into shoe leather for dinner, accompanied by a scoop of applesauce.

He explained that raw meat would give me worms—which was the answer to all my dieting prayers and woes. Every chance I got, I would consume anything that might give me a tapeworm, including Grandma's moldy lemonade.

My mother became concerned after she found me shoving a random chunk of raw hamburger meat in my face while hanging over the sink. She always had a way of understanding what I was doing, shaming me for it, and deliberately failing to accept any responsibility for her role.

In spite of my efforts to catch a tapeworm, I did lose a few extra pounds of water weight at my mother's favorite beach for communing with Ra.

And we both knew we were doomed when my mother emerged from her bedroom, smelling of weed and patchouli, and wearing her soft, velveteen pink bikini which hugged every curve—like my sister, Anna, her figure was the perfect hourglass. I could never carry the look as a short-waisted, long-legged girl whose hourglass had lost time in the mentally implanted imperfections hurled at me.

I didn't share much with my little brother Jason outside of our contempt for my mother's causeway beaches and the many hours we had to spend there.

However, my sister shared in my mother's exhibitionist spirit and sprinted to find the bikini that my mother had bought for her. However, Anna's bikini had been purchased at Belk's—a store that catered to the geriatric shopper and not the perfect hips that my sister possessed. As for me, I was not allowed to wear a bikini until I lost enough weight in my stomach to carry my frame, or so I was told.

The five-minute warning would be announced, and we would all load up *The Brick* with me and my siblings and a small, faded, red-and-white Playmate cooler with soggy PBJs heavily soaked in the warmed oils from peanut butter.

Naturally, those oily sandwiches were accompanied by Grandma's borrowed canteen filled with bitter Wyler's knock-off Kool-Aid. Also packed tight in the cooler were a few cans of Hamm's beer that nearly prevented it from closing entirely which could lead to leaking and skunked beverages. My mother's favorite beer was Coors, but it was hard to get because it was available only in certain places near the Colorado Rockies. You had to know someone who could bring the beer to you where you lived.

Rolling down the windows in *The Brick* did little to cool things down when the air blowing through was in the upper 90s to low 100s. It felt like someone was running a hair dryer on high heat in your face.

My mother's idea of quelling tempers was always to turn up the dial on the radio. Most days, she reached for her eight-track of "Hot Blooded" by Foreigner, which, interestingly, led to even more physical and verbal altercations between all of us.

It was official—my mother was on permanent vacation thirty years before she should have been, and her kids were along for the ride.

Growing up going to the beach may sound like a dream come true for most kids, but these were not the shores where you wanted to build a sandcastle. These were the kind of shores where the materials found in the sand were better suited for a halfway house or a brothel.

Ben T. Davis Beach was located along Causeway Boulevard and was far away from the fairy-tale beaches where tourists shuffled their feet for sand dollars and fed French fries to the seagulls that would have been just as happy to take a turd from their hand. Seagulls are perhaps the most ungrateful fowl on earth—they would shit on you whether you were kind enough to share your food offerings or were a local who never did.

Dad, Grandma, and Papa never came along with us to Ben T. Davis Beach. They were holding out for a trip to Fort De Soto Park, which was another forty-five minutes drive time—but it was devoid of the cigarette butts, hypodermic needles, and seedy walks of life.

My first introduction to Ben T. Davis Beach was certainly a shock. We had always vacationed in Florida, but we never stopped at the beaches along the way that lined the side of highway with cement shelters, picnic tables, and hatchbacks of cars open to traffic and smog.

My mother quickly found a pseudo-parking space near one of the lifeguard stands that backed up to the parking lot. Apparently, she was once a lifeguard and decided we would all be safer if we set up camp near them.

If I had complained about the heat of the car, I should have held my contempt for the sand. It was so fucking hot that walking on its surface would have caused severe third-degree burns. Instead, we all kept our flip-flops on, with the exception of my mother, who, it turned out, hated to go into the water or anywhere near it. Instead, she preferred to lie on a blanket, slathered in baby oil, with a fresh can of beer. She would even consume additional beta carotene from one of Cannidy's medicine cups to ensure that she was getting the most savage tan possible.

I could still spot our yellow, gingham blanket strategically placed far away from any shade and in close proximity to the lifeguard stand.

However, the best beacon was the light reflecting off my mother's mirrored, crotch-watching sunglasses which blinded everyone who dared to make eye contact with her. She was stretched out, reading a novel, and sipping on a beer in a koozie that fully concealed her adult beverage.

She also had her tanning timer going. Some months back, she had collected enough proof of purchases from boxes of Rice-a-Roni and sent away for a free kitchen timer that looked like the iconic San Francisco cable car. Every four minutes, it would play the jingle that had made the boxed side dish famous in commercials— "Rice-a-Roni, the San Francisco Treat"—and she would turn over to ensure that she had the most even tan. This was also a good time to apply more Hawaiian Tropic as she made friends with the sun and the lifeguards.

I have since lived in the San Francisco Bay area and can say with confidence that Rice-a-Roni is not considered the San Francisco Treat.

Near our beach blanket, my little brother was re-purposing a pile of smothered More cigarette butts as building materials for his castle.

After getting bored playing frisbee, my sister and I decided to venture into the water. The temperature felt like a balmy, microwaved Velveeta cheese product, and the trip from the blanket to the water's edge was treacherous and filled with the detritus of a debauched lifestyle.

Not many people enjoyed frolicking in the hot water, which could have doubled as a lab incubator for growing a plethora of bacteria. The only people in the water that day were a group of late teens or early adults. They were young and could have easily been tenants at the park. Circling the only female in the group were three guys who apparently were pissing off this gal, as her voice slowly gained in volume. I wondered if she was in the trouble the way that girls always were on TV until we heard her repeatedly shout, "Get away from me. I'm trying to take a shit."

My older sister Anna heard her loud and clear, and we both made a break for the shore and the sun's reflection off my mom's crotch watchers.

It was the last time we ever went in the water at a causeway beach.

CHAPTER 16

My Mother's Best Friend Is a Hooker

TRISHA LOOKED EXACTLY like the Malibu Barbie doll that I got for my fifth birthday. Malibu Barbie was the first of many Barbie dolls that I unintentionally maimed. Malibu met her demise due to airbrushed tan lines that were marketed to young girls.

Like my favorite Barbie, Trisha's soft-brown, long-flowing hair perfectly hung down the middle of her back—so thick that I would always imagine its weight affecting her posture and ability to use the toilet.

My Saturday nights and occasional day trips to those scummy local causeway beaches are strongly connected with the Pointer Sisters' hit "I'm So Excited" and the presence of Trisha. However, Trisha never had the privilege of an outing to Ben T. Davis.

My mom told me that she was part American Indian, which accounted for her naturally tanned skin, ridiculously thick hair, and a raging drinking problem. Trusted tenant Steve Winters was her main squeeze, for better or worse. They spent many years together, which you could consider lucky or cursed for Steve.

My first writings at the age of nine were my imagined accounts of competing against her in my fabricated beauty contests. I always lost in the swimsuit category because of my thick midsection. In my third-grade reality, it was not her long tanned and toned legs that would give me a run for my money for the title of the Most Beautiful Girl in the World contest—it was her mannerisms. Faked or not, even her sneeze was adorable and was a cross between a hamster fart and a rabbit squealing in delight.

Trisha didn't live in the park but would often keep Steve's bed warm, and during the day, she would swing by the house to hang out with my mom.

During the years that Trisha and Steve were together, I would lie awake either to the saturation of sweat on my calico-cat pillow that my Grandma Cavallari made me or the static over the radios of the Tampa Police Department officers who were standing in my kitchen. I learned not to be alarmed over the years because Steve and Trisha liked beer and brawls.

One night, Steve showed up for dinner. He had polished off a two-liter of Jolt Cola. He must have gotten up to take a dump or pee one hundred times in one hour. After he left, Anna, Jason, and I concocted a scheme to get our hands on the caffeine-infused serum that would keep us up late.

But it was a different kind of coke that got Steve into the most trouble. Legend has it that it took five cops to take him down one night. And every time Steve or any other tenant got into trouble, law enforcement and other emergency personnel knocked on our door.

The next morning, while Steve was still locked up for assault and battery against an officer, Trisha swung by to recount her version of the story. My siblings and I were sent out into the yard to play.

Like clockwork, Florence pulled up in her land barge of a vehicle and knocked down the trash cans. She was doing her best to not tip over while walking sideways and squinting against the glare of God's flashlight. As usual, we placed our bets that she would fail to acknowledge three kids in our shared yard, either deliberately or out of ignorance. At this point, we had been making mud pies and double-daring each other to trip her for four years.

Florence found her balance on the two steps leading to her front door and repeated the cycle of dropping her keys while trying to get the timing right to insert said key into the door lock—this was normal. She finally made contact and, in one motion, stumbled over the threshold and slammed the door behind her.

My little brother was his usual pain-in-the-ass that day, and, after destroying the Barbie water park we had created out of his old Hot Wheels Speedway loop tracks, we ditched him outside in our unfenced yard. My guess is he was around six because it was the year after the disappearance of Adam Walsh and our childhood innocence.

Trisha walked out just in time to grab my little brother before he was abducted by a local twenty-year-old convicted child molester named Kendall. The next morning, the static in the kitchen tolled for us. After that, I learned about perverts, pedophiles, and that Trisha was a good person in spite of practicing the world's oldest profession.

By the mid-'80s, Steve and Trisha had permanently parted ways. I never forgot Trisha or her signature sneeze. I was thankful that she was in our lives and there that day to protect my brother.

CHAPTER 17

Godfather's Lot

BEFORE TRISHA rescued my little brother from a near abduction by a child molester, before Florence came home stinking of Hamm's beer and Jade cologne, there was Godfather's Bar.

The former destination for bar flies and bar brawls, Godfather's now sat in a crumple of ruins consisting of broken beer bottles and shopping carts stuffed with comforters covered with filth and corn-blue flowers. It was the perfect set for the music video "The Land of Confusion" by Genesis.

Godfather's emptiness happened within two years of moving into the park. It sat just one ditch away from our backyard and became a good spot to shoot off bottle rockets and other fireworks illegally and openly obtained from white tents that popped up along roadsides during the Fourth of July or New Year's Eve holidays.

Over the course of five years, the same surly characters who were patrons of this drinking establishment came home to roost. The TPD were not just called to the park—they were often called to arrest the riffraff that hung out in this parking lot like zombies returning to a forgotten life.

Getting rid of Godfather's had been the biggest crusade of the houses surrounding the park even before we moved in.

Finally, capitalism came to the rescue and around the time that Laura Branigan was losing her "Self Control," the convenience store chain The Farm Store bought the property with the promise of offering shelves stocked with corn nuts, candies, and overpriced loaves of stale bread.

For several months, the sound of construction was welcomed. Word on the street was that free candy and goody bags would be part of the grand-opening festivities.

On a Sunday sunny afternoon in March of 1983, The Farm Store franchise flung open its doors on Hillsborough Avenue, complete with a rainbow-colored, inflatable hot-air balloon floating on the roof and samples of hard-as-a-rock ice cream and free Now & Later candies.

The rumblings also reached the only other kid our age living within a two-mile radius of the park, Matthew Meadows.

Matthew was two years older than me and lived with his grandparents on the outskirts of lot 5. I met Matthew when I was just six, and he was my first crush. He had a strange obsession with the song "The Devil Went Down to Georgia" by the Charlie Daniels Band. Matthew would typically show up in our driveway with three items: a Sony tape player, a cassette tape filled with "The Devil Went Down to Georgia" on both side A and side B so that he didn't have to rewind it, and the board game Risk.

Sarah and Samantha also came over for a sleepover that weekend to share in the freebies and fanfare. They remembered to bring their charms so we could trade which ones we really wanted. Frankly, I was tired of getting the tiny baby-bottle charm and had too many to count on several bracelets and necklaces.

Anna and Samantha were never searched or patted down to see how much free candy and ice cream they scored. However, Sarah and I knew our fate and were prepared to keep the amount of loot we had procured from the store's opening because the likelihood of it being confiscated was high, due to the diets our mothers had put us on. Samantha, Anna, and Jason were free to consume as much candy as their hearts desired. Matthew didn't like Now & Laters, so Sarah and I traded our ice cream for the candy. After all, candy was not perishable and was harder to track.

Matthew got to go to public school, and at least one of his parents was a police officer or at one time wore blue. He never talked about it, but his grandparents had full custody of him. Over the eight years that he was our neighbor, I never met them once, but I knew that they lived somewhere local. I wondered if they'd ever come to my house to arrest one of our tenants for drugs or beating up their girlfriend in one of our units.

I hated the board game Risk, but I loved that Matthew liked to play Risk because that meant we would spend hours together sitting on multicolored, webbed lawn chairs with the sound of country fiddles playing in the background.

On one particular sunny afternoon when I was nine years old, I felt that I had waited long enough, and I hit him with my best shot. I made my move by sliding in my mix tape compilation of love songs, leading with "Like a Virgin" by Madonna, followed by my biggest wooo, The Bangles' "Eternal Flame" as my final musical trapping. My maneuver to take over his territory and heart were defeated. He was infatuated with my sister, and in spite of this we remained friends. I couldn't blame him—Anna was full of life and didn't carry the weight or worry that I did.

The departure of Matthew was a big blow to our social life. Sarah and Samantha were still our closest friends, but they lived around fifteen minutes away, and Meredith's hours had changed since she'd picked up a few extra shifts at Frisch's. Their academics and sports schedule had also ramped up, so their days were often consumed with studying or volleyball tournaments. They were both gifted at the sport, and Mr. O'Connelly was an amazing coach.

One of the many rules of the park was that my parents didn't rent to families, so having any of our peers as neighborhood friends was not in the cards for us.

Helping to cushion the blow of the loss of Matthew's company was the arrival of Shanah, who was a teenager who had recently dropped out of high school and was living with her dad on lot 17. Because her living situation would be temporary, my parents bent the rules and allowed her to live in the park. She was only fifteen but already had a job at the mall at The Time Machine—a local arcade filled with my favorite games like Dragon's Lair, Burger Time, and Rampage.

Shanah always had gum, used the word "fuck" in every sentence, and wore super-tight Guess jeans and Coca-Cola brand baggy sweatshirts. Her mother was not in the picture, and, when I inquired about her whereabouts, she told me she didn't want to talk about her.

When she wasn't at work or at home with her dad, she would walk over and share her music collection and tokens from The Time Machine with me, Anna, and Jason. The game tokens were very appreciated, but my most coveted gift from her was a copy of her Sheena Easton album recorded onto a Memorex tape.

During the 1980s, I was forbidden to listen to Sheena Easton, Madonna, and the Beastie Boys. In fact, my mother and grandmother once made a trip to Tallahassee in the early '90s to picket against 2 Live Crew's lyrics arm-in-arm with Tipper Gore.

Meanwhile, while they held up signs in protest, I would run to my room digging through my underwear drawer to make sure that my most precious possession had not been confiscated. Some of my fondest childhood memories are of me and my sister screaming the lyrics to Sheena Easton's "Strut" into our hairbrush mircrophones and dancing wildly around the bedroom. Like all Memorex tapes, it met its demise from overplay, and, after a pencil was rendered impotent to reeling back in the ribbon, I laid it to rest.

After saying goodbye to my overplayed tape, three months later it was also time to say our farewells to Shanah. She didn't explain the reason for her sudden departure, but I did notice that her belly was much bigger and she hadn't been wearing her signature jeans anymore. She came to the park office to say goodbye with a half-gallon bucket filled with tokens as a parting gift.

CHAPTER 18
Steppin' Out

SATURDAYS WERE FOR swimming in Grandma and Papa's pool, followed by dinner out at The Red Apple located next door to the swankiest restaurant in town, Malio's.

Malio's was made famous thanks to the scandalous affair between Burt Reynolds and Loni Anderson in the early '80s. Often, I would stare through the glass doors of The Red Apple for a chance to catch them walking under the long, striped awning. Mostly, my curiosity was fixed on the parade of gold lamé, giant hair, black suits, and glamour.

We always occupied the largest booth in the smoking section. My parents and Papa always ordered coffee, and Grandma a sweet tea. The kids? Yeah, we got water. I longed for the taste of bubbly, artificial lime goodness to tickle my tongue or the chance to drink it so fast that it would set my nostrils on fire.

The kids' meals were the same: burger, chicken fingers, and your choice of a side that included applesauce, fries, or the soup of the day. But my mother worried about my weight, so, unlike Anna and Jason, I wasn't allowed to order fries.

We had the same waitress for several years, and we must have tipped her quite well, because she always greeted us with a smile even if we hung around for nearly two hours like campers.

The Red Apple at one time had a banquet room that was later converted and sold to a seafood restaurant called Clam Diggers and was a fave haunt of the portly Tom Seman. My parents hated seafood and were creatures of habit, so we tried the seafood place only once, thanks to Tom's appetite for BLT night.

One afternoon, lured to the house by the smell of bacon from his school-bus home, Tom devoured two pounds of crispy pork that was sitting out for bacon, lettuce, and tomato sandwiches. In his hour of embarrassment, he insisted that we finally dine at Clam Diggers on his dime.

The inside was mysteriously dark, with colorful neon signs adding to the ambiance. On a large wall, a fishing net hung clumsily with dusty seashells, starfish, and sand dollars forever trapped.

Random crab traps with plastic crustaceans inside hung above wooden lacquered tables. Since Tom was paying and Grandma wasn't there, we were allowed to order whatever we wanted. I promptly ordered a cheeseburger, a large order of fries, and a Sprite, which brought out a short and unexpected guttural belch from my throat and through my nostrils. Feel the burn.

CHAPTER 19

Dirty Oranges and Pineapple

SOMETIMES WISH we had been tenants paying lot rent in the park instead of dropped into an environment that was so drastically different from our daily surroundings. Our lifestyle, fate, and where we fit into society would have already been identified and accepted.

The failing public schools assigned to our address had an attendance rate of 58 percent Black, 17 percent Hispanic, 16 percent White, and 7 percent *Other*. Coupled with those dismal figures and a mishap during my time in kindergarten at Mendenhall Elementary in which I was sent to a school psychiatrist for anger issues, it was decided we would be enrolled in a private Christian school.

The first three years of my elementary education might have been my favorite. We attended West Hillsborough Baptist School, or WHBS. It was close to the house and just a mile or so from The Gold Minor, where the tenants liked to get falling-down drunk. The traditional white steeple stretching into the sky was out of place just around the corner from a dive bar and its sins inside, instead of the backdrop of some small, wholesome Connecticut town.

Each morning, I sat in a stuffy sanctuary, where we pledged first to the American flag, the Christian flag, and then the Bible. On a blackboard to the right, the weekend's Sunday school and church attendance were always dutifully recorded in chalk.

The ritual continued after taking a seat on a red-velveteen padded seat protecting long, creaky pews that were so worn from years of parishioners' asses shifting from side to side, it was more pink than red. More prayers and a message of sheer terror followed from the Old Testament. My introduction to the wrath of God yielded many nightmares that I still have on occasion.

Following a story of how Abraham nearly sacrificed his son to the Lord, I welcomed the recess and was ready to take a ride on the centurion of the playground, the slide. Towering at a treacherous height, its long, wavy path glistened and burned the retinas and asses of every child rider. Unlike today's plastic/petroleum impostors that had the nerve to be colored green, the slides of yesteryear were intermingled with pleasure, recklessness, and danger.

It was hard not to follow Jesus in a Christian school. Every bit of math, science, and social studies was peppered with parables throughout the textbooks. My mind often wandered, as it does for many kids sitting in class, to when the school supply store was open for business. Basically, the school supply store was a closet where elementary-age customers would stand in line to purchase Prang Crayons and 3½" × 5" poster cards with photo images of animals in peril.

The authority figures at school preached tales of being possessed by the devil if I listened to the Rolling Stones, or even worse, Michael Jackson. Some of the Christian schools were so strict that even the Christian rock band Stryper was off limits because they wore really tight pants and incorporated drums and guitars into their music. But mostly, it was their really, really, tight pants that I was reminded might stir up lust in my heart.

Still, that wasn't the biggest conundrum I faced. It was that my parents, their friends, and tenants in the park drank beer, smoked cigarettes, and listened to the devil's music. I had personally participated in all the evildoings by choosing to spin The Stones' album *Their Satanic Majesties Request*, among other taboo and disturbing album covers. Although, I never felt very evil dancing in the living room on the softness of our shag carpet to the guitar riffs of Pink Floyd or Freddy Mercury's iconic voice.

My mother had to remind me, when questions arose, that we attended these schools for their educational value because the public school system continued to fail us. Well, at least in our shitty neighborhood.

These Christian schools often had guest speakers who were also preaching at the church attached to the school. You know, kind of like snake-oil salesmen. One Monday morning I walked into the sanctuary, took my seat on the pink pads, and watched in bewilderment as a traveling minister pulled out a swimsuit that resembled my grandma's skirted, one-piece number from a large plastic caldron.

Instead of Shakespeare, we were to hear another tale of evil and lust. Yes, swimsuits were why females were raped, and males were driven to rape us because they listened to Gloria Estefan and Miami Sound Machine, and their eyes fed on our flesh. These messages were a running joke and anthem at the dinner table, but I still feared falling into hell in my dreams.

I quickly made friends with the "bad kids" or transplants who'd been raised outside of the church and didn't attend the church attached to the school. They were also there for the educational value that could be had—or the public school system simply was exhausted with their shenanigans. Either way, it felt good to be bad outside of my nightmares.

Most of the teaching staff still had beehive hairdos, while younger staff members went for the tight curled-perms—we called them "The Poodles." Students and their parents often rebelled at Halloween, which was a huge deal for WHBS. It was a miracle that they even acknowledged Halloween and didn't refer to the pagan holiday as a "fall festival." My parents were very creative and always made us the best homemade costumes.

In the early 1980s, store-bought costumes were unintentionally creepy and came with two crappy pieces: 1. a plastic mask that might suffocate you before the cheap strap snapped, and 2. a sort of vest or bib-like accompaniment to your ensemble. The rest was on you, so, most of the time, the parents called on a grandma to sew or got busy themselves trying to come up with a costume.

In third grade, I went as an FM/AM Walkman fashioned from a large cardboard box that once held one hundred rolls of toilet paper and tuning dials repurposed from an old Tonka truck that my brother no longer played with.

With a little spray paint and a dash of patience, I was transformed into the popular listening device. It's been my favorite Halloween costume to date, and I still think about making one for myself. I didn't take first place in the school's costume contest because my costume could, of course, promote listening to satanic music, but I took third place, and the yearbook staff (composed of middle-schoolers) chose to rewrite history by giving my costume its rightful place.

For all the effort that my parents put into our costumes, it was wasted on trick-or-treating. While our Halloween costumes might have kicked ass at school, we were forbidden to trick-or-treat the park or our neighbors surrounding the park. It was one thing to share a backyard with the tenants but it was a different story to take candy from them with great abandon.

Considering the numerous death threats and an abduction thwarted by Trisha, I could hardly blame my parents for being overprotective in this situation. And thanks to the scandals that plagued the news in the late '70s and '80s involving razors hidden in apples or poison injected into waxed-based candies, all confections were confiscated by my parents and examined before consumption.

We never received more than one or two trick-or-treaters at our front door, but Tom could be counted on to stare at my mother's ass or make some snarky comment about whether I had gained or lost weight even on Halloween.

By the third grade, my whole family, including Grandma and Papa, were all weighing in on my waistband, as well. Drive-thru Bob's wife, Alice, even offered to loan me her Richard Simmons Deal-a-Meal Cards to help me trim my waistline. Alice explained that she had ordered them one night while watching *Hardcastle and McCormick;* when a commercial for them came on, she knew she just had to have them. She claims that she lost at least four pounds and didn't need the cards anymore. My mother made the decision to allow me to borrow them, and, one week later, I promptly lost them … accidentally.

In spite of Tom's unwavering attention to my fluctuating pants size, he would bring over an offering of Hershey's bars and packs of Fruit Stripes—the chewing gum voted most likely to lose its flavor after just eleven seconds of mastication.

A few exceptions were made in the park, and we were permitted to head over to Steve Winters' and Cannidy's mobile homes and, of course, Drive-thru Bob and Alice's unit for homemade popcorn balls. However, given the track record of generosity extended to us through the kindness of the tenants at Placid Lakes, we were allowed to trick-or-treat Grandma's mobile home park.

The year was 1982, and every storefront and radio was blasting Vincent Price's haunting cackle from its tinny speakers. This was also the year that I met

Vic, Pineapple, and their mentally handicapped son, Daniel. Pineapple—or "Piney," as she was affectionally called—was a very short and very rotund woman of Polynesian descent with smooth, bronzed skin, a warm heart, and an infectious laugh. Vic was equally as short but thin, with large scars running down his chest from at least two heart surgeries of some sort. He also had an impressive collection of anything from the ad campaign for The California Raisins commercials.

He was an amazing cook thanks to his time in a federal pen for killing his first wife, who was responsible for Daniel's handicap and who took many lovers whom she made no effort to hide during their marriage. According to Vic, his first wife was Native American, beautiful, and cursed with the ugliness of alcoholism that caused Daniel's very cruel and severe mental retardation—or as it's called today, "intellectual disability." But in 1982, the more crude term existed and was used, even to his face. Daniel was physically eighteen years old but had the mind of a two-year-old and a kind of innocence that I understood at the age of just eight.

Vic, Piney, and Daniel were technically tenants at Placid Lakes, but they were treated as family—so much so, that like Grandma and Papa, they were just there. They were permanent fixtures at each and every celebration from birthdays to Thanksgivings held at Pelican Mobile Home Park or Placid Lakes. In fact, I was closer to them than I was to many blood relatives still living in Chicago.

Daniel would often accompany me and my siblings on the many adventures at Placid Lakes, including filling brown-paper grocery bags with dirty oranges plucked from the dozen or so trees, and borrowing books from the library closet where the strong smell of old newspaper and dusty pages were pungent and filled with mold spores. This same building also housed public showers, the laundromat, and an outdoor area where sagging clotheslines hung with the occasional unmentionables of octogenarians.

Every once in a while, we would score quarters from the coin-operated washers and dryers and, of course, the occasional candy bar from tenants.

Following a day of scouring for our spoils, we would head to dinner with the Gonzalezes at one of the many local feeding troughs and buffets that were named after old Saturday morning Westerns like Ponderosa Steakhouse or Bonanza. On occasion, we would hit more sophisticated dining establishments such as Morrison's, where the chopped steak and green beans were just the right amount of bland for kids and geriatrics.

Of all the places we patronized and my absolute favorite was part of an '80s restaurant-theme craze called "pizza and pipes." There was nothing bizarre about the cuisine, but the environment, in retrospect, was wonderfully unconventional.

While gnawing on a slice of cheese pizza, an organist in the center of the room told corny jokes and held singalongs to vaudevillian tunes while soap bubbles floated into the air and Buster Keaton films played on the backdrop of a movie screen.

My mom loved old films, and, outside of reading, it was the only thing I shared with her besides an umbilical cord. She tended to gravitate toward and dote on my little brother because of a shared personality and because he strongly favored my grandma's first husband—my mother's biological father. He was the grandfather who always sent us really expensive guilt gifts like Nikon cameras with pictures that I always destroyed because I would forget and expose the loaded film to the sunlight.

Our bond with the Gonzalezes was strong, and eventually Grandma hired Vic and Piney to manage the park and collect lot rents from the tenants after she bought a new park in Gibsonton, Florida. Around the time that I got my period and started seventh grade, Vic and Piney disappeared from our lives. I later learned that Piney was pocketing collected lot rents and, upon being fired by Grandma, left without a goodbye, taking with her my trust and faith in humanity.

CHAPTER 20

Giant's Camp

A LARGE DUST CLOUD shrouded the shabby eatery, caused by environmental factors such as dry gravel and the patrons who knew how to pull a good holeshot out of a parking lot. Giant's Camp Restaurant sat on Highway 41, marked by an enormous, size 22 decaying boot that belonged to a real man named Al "The Giant" Tomaini.

Al towered more than eight feet tall while his wife, Jeanie, was a mere two feet six inches in height. Jeanie's lack of stature was related to a birth defect that left her without legs. In spite of their differences—or because of them—the couple married and traveled the world as career sideshow performers or attractions, depending on who you ask in Gibsonton.

They managed to save enough money to retire early, adopt a few kids, and set up Giant's Fishing Camp and a cozy greasy spoon that was frequented by those in the carny business.

The first time that I had visited Giant's Camp Restaurant was four years earlier, when Grandma and Papa took me out for a messy burger after they bought a second mobile home park in the town of Gibsonton, or, as it's known by locals, Gibtown. The inside of the tiny establishment mirrored the outside—tired, small, broken-down but thriving.

The most peculiar thing about Giant's Camp Restaurant was that there was a dive bar located right inside the front door of the restaurant surrounded by black barstools, hanging onto duct tape for dear life, and a few electronic poker games.

Most mornings, evenings, and afternoons, each barstool would be filled with working-class folks on their way up from a bender and down from life. Because Milwaukee's Best was always flowing at the earliest hour that the law or its liquor license would allow, it barred patrons younger than twenty-one from that corner of the restaurant—but just that corner.

Black-and-white pictures of Al and Jeanie's adventures hung on the wall, paying homage to its founders. In particular, I liked sitting beneath the one of Al leaning inside a pen to pet a tortoise. The image intrigued me so much that I asked to meet him. Our waitress, Margaret, informed me that Al had passed away some time ago and Jeanie was still alive but seldom made an appearance.

Margaret was a short, round woman with kind eyes and an easy laugh who had worked at Giant's Camp Restaurant since she'd been in her twenties. She was around the same age as Grandma and always brought me chocolate milk at no charge even if Grandma objected. This immediately endeared her to me.

My Papa also had a fondness for Margaret and innocently flirted with her every time we came in. I did enjoy the food, but I also knew that, if I wanted to keep it that way, I would steer clear of the kitchen or the bathroom out back. Over a decade-plus of patronage, I can count on one hand how many times I used the restroom there, and, while I never spotted one, I was sure there had to be one of those wolf spiders tucked in the piping under the sink so thick with dust that it could have been mistaken for a tarantula.

Still, I had already amassed some pretty interesting memories to reflect upon from Giant's Camp before we even moved there. One Christmas when I was around nine, we got to see a drunk carny arrive in an air/sea plane dressed in a dirty Santa suit. The plane landed on the rickety dock that hung out over the Alafia River. Out stumbled Santa, his dishwater-colored beard stained from what was probably dishwater, with a sack full of small, unicorn-etched mirrors for the girls and stuffed orange owls for the boys.

I reluctantly sat under my favorite picture of Al and watched as a double Jack and Coke was slid over to him before he welcomed all the good kids who'd remembered to bring their lists. Not only did I forget my list, but I forgot whether I had been a good girl. Thanks to Santa's libations, he didn't remember, either, and I still got a unicorn mirror to take home.

Giant's Camp—or just "Giant's" to locals—would become our new Red Apple.

CHAPTER 21

Gibtown

A LARGE FERRIS WHEEL loomed taller than any mobile home or prefab house on the street, bursting with rainbow-glowing neon tubes turning in time to "Let's Dance" by David Bowie—the lack of riders causing each bucket to rock wildly.

It was also the kind of house with a plethora of warning signs about dogs hanging loosely fastened to chain-link fences and which sagged, much like Sarah and Samantha's fortress. The dogs, in this case, could have been canine *or* human.

At first, I thought there was some sort of street festival happening, like the ones I had attended with Sarah and Samantha at their Catholic school festivals and fairs. But the misplaced ride sat in the front yard of my Papa and Grandma's new neighbors and at the entrance of their recently acquired mobile home park, Chalet.

Typically, the word "Chalet" would bring up images of quaint Swiss villages nestled among snow-covered peaks. But Grandma and Papa's Chalet was a long, hard, rocky road that led to a circle of nine very neglected, single-wide mobile homes surrounding a rusty shed that had weathered many storms but could easily be knocked over by a quick breath.

An additional quarter-mile of large chunks of discarded concrete paved the way to Grandma and Papa's new home—a single-wide trailer infested with wolf spiders. Grandma's theory was that raised potholes deterred speeders by slowly killing the alignment and axles on most vehicles.

Wolf spiders are not poisonous, but they can bite. I never felt the sharp pain from their fangs or was even certain that they had them, because the mere presence of these little bastards sent me running at least one mile from where I found them.

The arachnids in Grandma and Papa's mobile home were around an inch in length, and—I swear by all that is holy—I could spot them at night by sweeping the room with a flashlight and catching the shine of their eyes. When discovered, they would jump into the darkness and straight into my nightmares.

I never did get over my fear of spiders, but my Papa's afternoon naps would often calm my nerves while I would stay with them and my arachnid friends. On his nightstand, he kept a small transistor radio and a white, plastic oscillating fan that softly blew the curtains open while his Easy Listening station played. Without fail, "Captain of Her Heart," by the one-hit Swiss duo Double, would play through the small speaker and the thought of sleeping with my flashlight clutched like a Jedi would fade away.

Gibsonton—or "Gibtown," as it is affectionately known by locals—is the self-proclaimed carny capital of the world by those working in the business. In fact, Gibtown has special zoning exceptions for homeowners so that ferris wheels, corn-dog stands, and tilt-a-whirls can sit smack dab on your front lawn.

Thanks to all that time spent slurping up greasy burgers and syrupy chocolate milk at Giant's, I was able to brush up on carny lingo and better understand Papa and Grandma's second home.

Carny Glossary:

24-Hour Man—The employee assigned to the boring task of directing cars into the parking lot with a shabby arrow sign.

86'ed—Banned from the lot. This could apply to those thrown out for lack of cash or abundance of alcohol in or on them and actual carnival employees as well.

A&S Man *a.k.a.* Guess Your Weight/Fool the Guesser— These were the unfortunate fools you hoped would guess your weight or age incorrectly. Either way, they won, because the cost to play was larger than your weight or age.

Advance Man—This is the guy who would most likely grease the palms of local politicians to set up the carnival as well as put sponsors in place before the show arrived.

Mark—People who attended the carnivals—in particular, the arcade, where the games are located. The term "mark" comes from the early days of boardwalks, where those who could be fooled into spending money on fixed games would literally have their backs marked with chalk.

Agent—The best rigged-game operators who knew how to sell a mark on playing and beating the odds for a win. Typically, they would be paid more than their counterparts on less-skilled games that required the least amount of persuasion.

Alibi Store—A clever excuse that an agent will use to keep you playing the "rigged" game.

B.C.—Stands for "Be cool." Basically, you need to chill out with whatever you are doing at the moment, because it's more than likely illegal or could get you into trouble.

Back End—The place where the best games and rides are strategically placed at the back of the carnival to keep you there longer. Kind of like how your local grocer puts the dairy aisle and other staples farthest from the front door.

CHAPTER 22

Waste Management

HATED TUESDAYS AND Thursdays but Tuesdays even more. These were the days of the week that we collected trash from the tenants.

The summer of 1984 was the season that we got our feet wet as garbage collectors.

Negotiations with Waste Management Services did not go well, and a heated dispute played out over an avocado-colored phone over the spike in costs and a required dumpster that my parents refused to lease for the park. My mother slammed down the receiver so hard that the ringer inside rattled—back when slamming down the phone with force and without hesitation was possible.

It was decided that we would carve out the cost of trash collection and that the physical burden and smell would be placed on me, Anna, and Jason.

My parents were convinced that we were dealing with mobsters, and, like Tony Montana, they had no plans of backing down. We never had to play rough, but my parents often forgot that they weren't pushing corn nuts at the local liquor store and that WMS didn't give a shit if we ended up playing garbage man in our half-occupied mobile home park.

Lifting the metal lid from the can, you would be always be met with the smell of wet, skunked lager that had sprung from the leak of a cheap trash bag. We're talking a whole weekend of douching, shooting up, hairbrush dander, fried foods, and rotting meats and meals.

These forms of detritus were the perfect breeding ground for flies. In one fell swoop, my preschool memories of lifting a lid and encountering a surly, green puppet were shot to shit.

In spite of my parents informing the tenants to always use trash bags, never directly place trash into the metal cans, and separate aluminum cans, most did whatever the hell they wanted.

While my mother drove our newly acquired, white 1983 Chevy pickup, we jumped out of the idling vehicle and lifted the lids off the silver trash cans and dumped the waste into the bed of the truck.

Gary, on lot 6, was the worst offender. He would simply dump mounds of crushed Hamm's beer cans, used diabetic needles and catheters, among other abused medical supplies, and unfinished Hungry Man dinners directly into the cans.

Ralph and Vivian's trash on lot 4 contained so much grease and gelatinous sludge that the lid and all the contents were too slippery to handle. Ralph suffered from high cholesterol and heart disease, and eventually ended up with a pacemaker. We were convinced that Vivian was trying to kill him off with a daily diet guaranteed to clog the healthiest of arteries. Following his second triple bypass, we discovered two severely damaged skillets with at least five inches of white-speckled, hardened lard inside.

Call it poverty lines or laziness, other short- and long-term tenants followed suit, and anything from discarded douche bottles to pork chop bones were dropped indiscreetly and directly into the metal receptacle. Ironically, Florence's trash was pretty tidy in comparison, and she went through the trouble of using an actual trash bag to contain her half-eaten TV dinners and empty bottles of booze.

After loading up the truck, we all squeezed into the cab sans seatbelts and followed the squawking of soaring sea gulls. The stench of the transfer station was often overlooked because we'd already been stewing in the smell of the tenants' waste for a good twenty-minute drive.

Going to the dump on a regular basis meant that we knew everyone who worked there on a first-name basis. They even greeted my mother with "Norm!" like she was the character on the television show *Cheers* who was a regular at the bar.

Because the dump station was not open yet, the trash rode with us to school, unlike in the summer months, when we had to wait in the truck while my mother did the unloading and hosed it out while seagulls screamed overhead.

Citing social suicide, my sister would, on occasion, win the battle of getting my mom to switch vehicles and leave the dump truck at home and drop us off at school

in *The Brick* instead. But most of the time, the tenants'
trash accompanied us through the carpool lane.

When you hit puberty as a girl in Christian schools,
the burden of sexual attraction from the opposite sex
was your cross to bear and yours alone. It was a forced
acceptance to what was going on in spite of the fact
that your emotions were lagging behind your body's
development.

The new school was Heritage Christian School.
Unlike WHBS, special attention was given to what you
wore by Principal Charles Smith, or, as we liked to
call him, "Principal Smiley," or just "Smiley" for short.

Principal Smiley always wore a dark suit, black
slicked hair secured and plastered with hair spray,
and a wide, permanent grin that exposed his sparkling
white teeth. Each morning, he would devote his time
to prayer and pinching the legs of middle-school girls
to confirm that we were wearing panty hose in the
obvious absence of socks.

Skirts that were questionable in length and didn't
at least reach the middle of our wobbly knees would
lead to "the kneel test." Wherever you stood, be it a
concrete floor or a carpeted classroom, your virtue
would be challenged. If your skirt didn't hit the ground

following genuflecting, your parent would be phoned for a change of clothes and a demerit issued. It was commonplace to see a girl somewhere in front of the chapel, church office, or playground kneeling in front of Smiley.

We were dressed in our Sunday best for school before the arduous task of tossing the pungent detritus into the back of the truck. My mother always blasted music from the cab to keep us motivated. This morning, it was her favorite, "Neutron Dance," by the Pointer Sisters.

After losing a game of roshambo to my siblings, I was stuck with lot 6. Gary's weekend had been filled with injury and reckless abandonment, and, in my haste to be done with his waste, I failed to smooth my skirt before boarding our dump truck for school.

Smiley made a beeline for my legs this morning, as I had decided to forgo wearing socks. He was met with scraped knees, a short hem, and a maggot—lesson learned.

CHAPTER 23

Wicked

HAD BECOME A BIT rebellious as I inched closer to puberty. My recent shenanigans involved sneaking a pack of Pall Malls from my mom's cigarette carton that she kept in the fridge next to the Wyler's puckered-flavored lemonade. Unfiltered Pall Malls were considered some go-to-hell smoking by most smokers, and, due to the harshness, I could never ready my throat for the burning while inhaling.

My mother discovered my crime in the bottom of my purple Jordache purse, squeezed in next to my Bubble Gum Kissing Potion. She addressed it by openly humiliating me in front of a group of adults—or any bystander within earshot—by asking me to pay her for the pack I stole—which I did and, by my own volition, decided not to keep.

My second act of rebellion was of grave concern to the Christian school I attended in fifth grade. I was gunning for principal's honor roll and had all As and one measly B in math. Back then, grades were actual letters and were released on a handwritten report card, in ink.

My teacher, Mrs. Metzger, changed her mind about my math grade without sharing this information with me or on my progress report. She later explained that she had a change of heart about the timeliness of when I turned in my classwork and felt that, by reducing my grade on my actual report card, it would teach me to work harder and learn a valuable lesson. Mrs. Metzger didn't like me, and the feeling was mutual.

After already celebrating my academic accomplishment at Showbiz Pizza, I refused to further endure the shame and changed what I felt was an undeserved grade on my report card.

I had completely forgotten my crime until a few months later, when Mrs. Metzger released the new report card grades. With a swift yank of my arm, I was pulled from my desk and reluctantly dragged to Smiley's office. Mrs. Metzger explained what I had done, how she was very concerned about my soul, and with God as her witness, blamed the devil for my deviant behavior. I assured her that the decision was solely mine and that it had not occurred to me to consult the devil.

At home, I was forced to pay off my debt for a celebratory night at Showbiz using the funds that I had saved up for a new set of slinky bracelets at Floriland Mall. At school, Principal Smiley attended to my spiritual health by delivering three swift swats to my ass and daily lessons in his office, where we would pray for my soul and pore over Bible verses. One of my least favorite exercises was when he would use a mirror, and I would have to study my reflection to find the good in my eyes.

The counseling left me traumatized and quite changed. I was thirty-three years old before I could even stand to watch a trailer for the film *Something Wicked This Way Comes*, and I have never seen the film.

In spite of what occurred, I officially made honor roll again and managed to survive the end of fifth grade, no thanks to Mrs. Metzger, Smiley, the devil, or the Bible.

CHAPTER 24

United Skates of America

As a rule, skating rinks, no matter where you grew up, looked exactly the same, with the same cast of characters, such as the loser DJ who never plays requests, guys too old to hang out at a skating rink, and every surface upholstered in dank carpet with years of soiled soda in the fibers.

The summer before my sixth-grade year, I spent quite a bit of time raging at the rink because that's where my crush and classmates from fifth grade spent their time.

I was feeling particularly psyched after gaining some popularity and notoriety due to my grade-changing scandal.

Like most prepubescents, I needed music on at all times to bring out my mood and connect with my identity.

On the corner of my dresser, a rather weak radio signal was producing a staticky sound through my pink boombox speakers as I got ready. Casey Kasem's cheesy voice was indexing American Top 40, and I had my mix tape loaded with my fingers poised and ready to hit the play and record button at just the precise moment to capture Michael McDonald's "Sweet Freedom."

Casey had teased the song earlier in his broadcast, linking the song and artist to the Doobie Brothers and another hit with Patti LaBelle, "On My Own," which was released to create the right mood for people my parents' age while they cozied up on the couch with Riunite.

Earlier in the day I had captured the perfect sound recording of Huey Lewis and the News' "Power of Love," sans the DJ talking over the intro.

The first time I had heard the hit was when Grandma had taken me, Anna, Sarah, and Samantha to see *Back to the Future* at the dollar theater. I was so moved by the performance of Alex P. Keaton that I had replaced all my *Teen Beat* posters of Kirk Cameron with Michael J. Fox.

Standing in front of a full-length mirror in a half-shirt, I was desperately trying to smooth the curled corners of my iron-on across my flat chest so that my shirt read, "lil' angel" instead of "lil' ang."

In spite of the wear and tear, it was my favorite shirt because of the color, and because my mother would never have approved of me wearing anything risqué because she felt I didn't have the build or body for it—another more subtle act of defiance.

I had lost most of my pudginess following a growth spurt, and my limbs began to take on a long, lanky appearance. I had also stopped getting a pixie cut every time my mom took us to Fantastic Sam's and my hair had finally passed my shoulders—an exercise in patience for me.

In the mirror, my reflection revealed the perfect poof with just the right volume in the center of my forehead framed by curled, winged-back hair. The breeze emitted from my standing plastic fan was no match for my Aussie Sprunch Spray. Over the years, I couldn't get my hair to hold a perm no matter how many chemicals were used. My mother hated my pixie cuts, so she had no problem footing the bill for a spiral perm.

Instead, I turned to curling irons and hair sprays that had so much lacquer it left behind white flakes in my hair when I applied too much.

In spite of the lack of pigment on my neck and an eyebrow that was half-white in color, I was feeling like tonight was the night Kevin Gallagher would ask me to couples-skate. And if I was lucky, I could get the DJ to take my music request and play "Lost in Your Eyes" by Debbie Gibson.

I cinched the drawstring on my generic Jams closer to my body in a feeble attempt to further flatten my stomach. Jams were knee-length, colorful shorts that signaled the end of the short-shorts of the late '70s and early '80s and ushered in an era of knee-length poopy-assed apparel—which I still protest a bit to this day. I mean, I didn't throw up all those calories for nothing.

Jams—or rather Jams prints—were usually wild, splashy images darting away from the direction of fashion and landing on the laps of the misinformed youth with parents with billfolds. Rest assured, Grandma would see to it, with her sewing and shopping skills, that those billfolds did not take a hit. Thankfully, she didn't drag us all to the K-Mart for another Blue Light Special stampede that nearly killed us all one Christmas after Grandma bought us all a pair of parachute pants.

I had to look good for Kevin, and, since the school year was coming to an end, it was my chance to make my move.

Unlike my hair that had to be forced against its will to hold a curl, Kevin's hair was soft and blond, and held the perfect wave. He had also excelled at every sport he had tried since he was three, and he wore real, brand-name Jams. His dad was a pilot for Eastern Airlines and was a regular and expected speaker on Career Day.

I liked him and many others like him for shallower reasons, but I later discovered my attraction would always be short-lived because depth can only form when what is desired is unattainable in spite of effort.

I drew a deep breath, walked out the door in my half-shirt, knock-off Jams, generic bo-bos, and crunch-infused hair spray. I was ready.

My dad dropped me off, so I was able to slink out of the house in my inappropriate half-shirt. The skating rink was packed, and I was thankful to own my own pair of Riedell black speed skates purchased with money from mowing the lawns of the tenants for three-dollars-a-pop. It was my favorite purchase next to the Pogo Ball that I had saved a whole summer to buy.

Renting the standard, ugly-brown boots with the orange stopper dropped your coolness factor to negative numbers. Renting speed skates was certainly respected but cost extra and was not included in the entry fee into the rink. Plus, foot fungus was likely thriving inside the boot.

I slipped on my skates and took a quick lap around the rink, looking for a familiar face. Sarah had promised to show up that night. We had seen less and less of her and Samantha as their educational and extracurricular demands increased. Samantha was missing due to some volleyball tournament.

I scanned the colorful wall of lights blinking in time to Morris Day and The Time's "Jungle Love" which Sarah and I liked to joke was the "Oreo, Oreo" song. There was no sign of Kevin, and I pictured him at home and in a neighborhood that was missing a surly old woman who was always three sheets to the wind.

Sarah finally showed up just in time to do the hokey pokey—a skating-rink staple that she relished and I detested. As usual, she talked me into it. Turning in a circle, I made silly faces and rolled my eyes as I put my whole body in and wished I had opted out. Of course, this is when Kevin decided to make an appearance with his entourage of fellow soccer-team pals.

I'm pretty sure he didn't see me, and I made a break for the snack bar. Sarah rolled off the rink and onto the carpet behind me. She knew all about Kevin and the importance of this evening. On the other side of the rink, Kevin and his crew headed over to play Asteroids. I wanted him to notice me, so I made sure I skated to my favorite songs like Roy Orbison's "You Got It."

Turns out, the only song that could compete with Asteroids was "Beat It" by Michael Jackson, and Kevin took to the skating rink, taking turns as fast as possible. He was a good skater, but because he preferred video games to the rink, he was not as fast as I was.

Sarah and I took turns trying to see if I could finally get his attention—but, just like in class, he failed to notice me. After many whispering sessions in the bathroom, we heard the DJ announce the last song of the night, which was also the couples skate. In a hurry, I bolted out of the bathroom and headed over to the

Asteroids game. Kevin finally noticed me, but for the wrong reason. Trailing at least ten feet behind me and attached by what I hoped was water, not urine, was a long banner of single-ply toilet paper.

I skated away, and Sarah helped me to remove the toilet paper, which had become entangled in my left wheels. I could still hear Kevin and his friends laughing and Debbie Gibson crooning about "... *getting weak from just a glance ....*"

Waiting until I was sure the entire skating rink had cleared out, I met my dad, who was fuming over how long it took me to finally come outside. I explained what had happened, and he gave me a tight hug and shared similar horror stories of embarrassment.

I was thankful for a dad and a good friend who reminded me of my worth, and that Kevin would not be returning to my school the following year.

CHAPTER 25

You're All Gonna Die

THE ONLY THING separating us from the tenants was a layer of particleboard and lifestyle choices. Hanging on the back of the great divide was a target that my mother had used at the local gun range, riddled with bullet holes in the chest and head. I grew up with no fewer than three guns at one time in our home—all of them unregistered to anyone in our household and loaded. They included one .38-caliber revolver and two 12-gauge shotguns.

We were taught that both would blow our legs off and render us unable to go to the skating rink ever again. It was easy to believe, since Gary and other tenants were missing limbs, even if those injuries were due to medical neglect and stupidity.

The 486 square feet of space housed the park's office, some storage, cleaning supplies, and my dad's workshop space, where he kept a pack of Freshen-Up gum in his tool chest.

My dad's woodwork shop included a lathe, table saw, and a Tradesman round channel vise—all of which could have doubled as torture devices and were intimidating enough. The table saw sat on a layer of mildewed, maroon-colored carpet left over from my dad's project carpeting the walls of *The Brick* in the late '70s.

It was also where my dad liked to hide his stash of strawberry-filled-center hard candies. Other random shit strewn about in his workplace once included a sliver of yellow soap that resembled a chunk of forgotten cheddar cheese. I know this because I took a bite out of it after my sister dared me.

A flimsy, makeshift wall divided the desk, storage space, and workshop. The storage area was a pile of random cleaning equipment, including a carpet shampooer that I loved to pretend was a scooter.

Squeezing the handle led to the release of a mixture of water and chemicals.

Disorder ruled our household. There were always stacks of mail, laundry, and dishes. In fact, our dishwasher was a rolling receptacle and had to be installed via hoses to the faucet—by an adult, of course.

Like the vise in my dad's workshop, the dishwasher was industrial-strength, and opening it following a cycle could result in severe injuries like melting the skin off your face, similar to the scene in the film *Indiana Jones: Raiders of the Lost Ark* where the Nazis dared to look upon the Ark of the Covenant. Hey, we were warned and had it coming.

Before evictions were served in a court of law, the whole family was on alert for the possible violent repercussions that would follow.

The time leading up to eviction for nonpayment of rent was not the worst, but it brought out the worst in tenants. Before Drive-Thru Bob started as Park Manager back in 1983, we would be instructed to stay out of the office and in our rooms. We took these commands seriously after witnessing several tenants knock on our front/office door and ask for our parents, only to eavesdrop on a conversation about how they would burn us all alive, starting with the children.

My parents could always smell danger and met them at the door packing heat. My mother liked to carry the .38 in the back of her cut-off jeans and orange Buccaneers jersey, and my dad casually carried the 12-gauge in his left hand. You know, like a nice bottle of chianti.

CHAPTER 26

TGIF

SARAH AND SAMANTHA were never available anymore for sleepovers or even just the occasional afternoon of chasing Duchess around the yard and getting a dipped cone at Bo's Ice Cream.

Following a sudden transfer to a new Christian school in sixth grade, my siblings and I were once again forced to adapt to a new school, teachers, friends, and environments. I was always concerned about the crime-and-punishment policy for students over the friendliness of the teachers.

This was the year that Anna and I met the Mitchell sisters. Like Sarah and Samantha, they were almost the same age, with the major exception that they lived in what I considered a normal house in a subdivision with neighbors that had kids and adults who hadn't done hard time or hung out at a bar notorious for drug raids.

Jennifer and Stacy, along with their Cleaver-esque mom, all battled their waistline, but their approach was more practical. Instead of shame, they admitted to their love of good food and affinity for unhealthy eats and put on a VHS tape of Jane Fonda in the living room to offset for the caloric intake.

Their pantry was lined with Cocoa Puffs, Count Chocula, Fruit Loops, and a plethora of salty snacks. Potato chips and soda were all within our reach and encouraged on the occasion of sleepovers.

Which was the other reason that my friends never wanted to spend the night at our house. Our pantry was lined with cans of creamed corn, sliced canned mushrooms, and cereals, from Malt-O-Meal to Puffed Rice to the equally bland Puffed Wheat. I hovered around my BMI mostly because I would have rather starved than eat that shit. Actually, I later developed a taste for the canned, slimy fungi.

Jennifer and Stacy's father was a software engineer with IBM and had a considerably high BMI. He seemed proud of it and boasted about opting out of Jane Fonda's living-room workouts.

If our sleepover was scheduled for a Friday night, we always went to the T.G.I. Friday's for dinner, and nothing was off limits, including soda, French fries, and appetizers. Most foreign to me and Anna was the idea of ordering anything before your dinner that might spoil it.

In the '80s, T.G.I. Friday's was *the* place for adults to hang out in suburbia. The servers wore "flares" or buttons on wacky suspenders and usually had some signature trick up their sleeves.

The bartenders were hired for more than their talent to mix a tequila sunrise or a grasshopper, which was Jennifer and Stacy's mom's favorite cocktail. They blew fire from their mouths using a little booze and flipped stainless steel shakers over the back of their heads like circus performers.

After snarfing down potato skins with heavy dollops of sour cream and several refills of soda, Mr. and Mrs. Mitchell ordered more fruity libations and ordered the four of us to the arcade nearby.

I remember reaching for my lawn-mowing stash of cash only to be stopped by Jennifer, whose dad had coughed up some dough to split among us. Like Sarah and Samantha's dad, he laughed easily and didn't seem bothered by the idea of spending money on enjoying life.

I loved every minute of this world and wanted to be a part of it, even if my parents argued that the homes were cookie-cutter and looked like everyone else's house.

We were lucky enough to enjoy their company and friendship for one school year, but, like the majority of the tenants in the park, they moved and slipped away from our lives, their fate unknown.

CHAPTER 27

Requiem for a Tenant

I T WAS THE THIRD TIME in the last month that the flashing lights raced across our living-room walls. The sound of snorting brakes from the emergency vehicles that lurched over the park's speed bumps was never a good sign. Tonight, at the ungodly hour of unrest, a knock. The usual uniformed Tampa Police Department officer stood in the doorway where I had watched a decade of tenants threaten to harm us.

It was Ralph again. The ambulance was on its way to lot 4, and again, Ralph's wife, Vivian, was hysterical. Ralph's frequent visits to the ER and bypasses had become so routine that the sense of alarm would no longer sound.

However, this was the third visit in one month, and years of grease-laden foods had finally brought Ralph to his knees. He was dead before he even made it on the gurney. Ralph's death was the first in the park and one of six that occurred before we moved away in the summer of 1989. Vivian was overcome with grief and moved immediately into an assisted-living facility after his passing.

Lot 4's new occupant was a surly fellow named James. Like many of the tenants in the park, James's vices had aged him an additional ten to fifteen years beyond his real age. His salt-and-pepper hair hung like tufted feathers around his flushed-pink temples and had multiplied in his ears and nose. James was semi-retired after an accident in a machine shop had left him nearly deaf.

Due to the considerable loss of hearing, he often left his television on at ear-shattering decibel levels. Early evening, as the twilight loomed, the theme to *Remington Steele* could be heard all the way to lot 31 at Steve Winters's mobile home, where he might have been throwing back Milwaukee's Best and bedding Trisha.

James was a bit of a loner, preferring to surround himself with Captain Stubing and Gopher or bear witness to a cross-examination with Matlock. Most of the other tenants didn't care for James. I could only half blame them. Who the hell wants to hear the theme to *Murder She Wrote* to the point of distortion 24/7?

When Tom wasn't waddling over to our house to stare at my mother nipping out, and snarfing down our bacon, he was reporting on James's whereabouts and other neighborly crimes being committed in the park. Tom would have liked to have become the park manager, but Drive-Thru Bob had the chops, and you couldn't really argue with an ex-Marine who was missing his trachea.

Over the next few months, we saw less and less of James, and Tom was otherwise occupied with reporting on other, more important issues such as mandatory hurricane evacuations for people living in mobile homes in Florida.

Tom wanted to be able to come and go from the shelters and take the PBJs with him, but emergency workers would not allow you to leave until cleared to go home. Other than James's television, this was the new issue that kept him up at night.

No one had noticed James leave his mobile home even for a quick beer run, but what they did notice were flies the size of Buicks buzzing and banging around the inside of the windows.

My mother was smart enough not to enter James's lot and called the TPD. An officer showed up once again on our doorstep. I was instructed to stay home and out of the way. This was ridiculous, because it could have easily been in our backyard and was next door to Florence's unit, which, technically, *was* our backyard.

I waited until my mother grabbed the keys to the unit and escorted the officer to James's windows, which were now blaring the voice of Judge Wapner carrying out a verdict on *The People's Court*. To this day, I wish I had never snuck around the corner because I smelled the recognizable stench of death hanging in the humidity of the day. In between the officer's retching, I overheard him ask, "Was your tenant a caucasian man?"

After the news that the only creatures that had been watching all those television shows in James's living room for the past two weeks had been flies, the tenants decided to hold a small vigil for their fallen brother. Not surprisingly, Tom was the one who organized a small gathering at his school bus for coffee, bear claws, and beer. Although my family was invited, we sent Drive-Thru Bob as our representative.

Three months later, on a hotter afternoon than the last, I came home from school and retreated to the backyard, where I heard moans coming from Florence's front steps. She had apparently been sitting shit-faced and sunburned for a few hours. Florence had not uttered more than three sentences to me in nine years, so I was shocked to have her call me over and ask me to send for my mother.

Drinking had distracted her from hygiene. Her skin was ashen—hair matted and greasy. What really got my attention was the fact that she had dried shit in-between her toes. I really wanted to further investigate how she even managed to ignore that amount of fecal matter before it had a chance to dry, but I realized I would not get a satisfactory or sane answer, anyway.

My mother called for an ambulance, but Florence refused to be transported to the hospital for further observation. A week later, her embarrassed adult daughter showed up for a rare visit at the urging of my mother. Her daughter exited the mobile home. She had found her mother dead on the toilet, and in the same clothes and maybe the same dried shit as when I had encountered her.

At the urging of Florence's family, no vigils or remembrances were to take place. Florence was a window of curiosity into my youth that had forever closed. I mourned this more than her presence.

My sister had her own reservations and theories surrounding the string of passings in the park. If the waves of demise continued in sequential order, our home would be next.

My parents had also had enough of the tenants, cops, ambulances, Lysol, and cockroaches.

I'm not sure why it took them almost a decade, but the decision to sell the park was a unanimous one within my family. Grandma, on the other hand, was not onboard. She felt that owning a mobile home park was a noble profession.

As for the rest of the tenants, some we kept in contact with, and others disappeared or migrated to other living arrangements.

Tom Seman eventually moved out of the park within a couple of years after we sold it and managed to get someone to marry him—basketball baby and all. He also returned to his computer-programming job and moved into his new bride's condo.

Hattie stayed relatively healthy in spite of her grave description of her everyday ailments. She did break her hip and made a full recovery, but her creepy son convinced her to move into his place with his girlfriend so he could suck her finances dry.

Harry pissed off one too many people. After a night out at The Gold Minor, he was shot dead after being accused of lifting jewelry from one of the regulars at the bar.

Gary stayed at Pelican Mobile Home Park up until his dying days in hospice care through the VA. True to his passion, he raised and kept cockatiels throughout the rest of his life.

Steve Winters still calls Pelican Mobile Home Park home and still owns his own unit, where he pays only the rent on the lot. He never saw Trisha again after their final fight, which turned physical. My parents check in with him from time and time, and Steve claims that his hell-raising days are over. Or, in his exact words after his last arrest, "I'm getting too old for this shit."

Trisha's low-key cocaine habit took a turn for the worse. We were told that she was living in a motel near

The Gold Minor with her pimp, who was supplying her with drugs. Her whereabouts are unknown. Out of all the tenants, I had the highest hopes for Trisha and was saddened by the news.

David and Donald's departure was not a loss but a huge relief to my mother and, frankly, the rest of the tenants. Apparently, David and Donald had complained to more than just my mom about being tracked for buying kiddie porn from overseas. My hope is that they found a new home somewhere in a prison cell.

Cannidy moved to the other side of Florida's coast, closer to Cocoa Beach, shortly after our departure. He bought a little cottage with a hot tub and is still a very close friend of my family.

Bob and Alice stayed on as mangers of Pelican Mobile Home Park for another seven years after we moved. Alice continues to rule the remote and plant deeper roots in her sofa.

My memories surrounding Pelican Mobile Home Park formed in the same way a scab does—each layer encasing and protecting the wound so that it's allowed to heal or fester, depending on the individual.

CHAPTER 28

Exodus

ONE NIGHT AFTER having dinner with Grandma and Papa at The Red Apple, my parents made the announcement on the way home that they planned on selling the park and leaving the mobile home park management game.

We had taken some major steps toward a better life starting with the purchase of a Mark III conversion van that had velveteen reclining seats, curtains to match, and real blinds for privacy. The velveteen took me back to our days at The Knights Inn, when we first moved into the park.

I wondered, like I had for the last nine-plus years, just how sweet life would be to live in a real neighborhood like Jennifer and Stacy.

Two weeks later, we had a potential buyer arriving for dinner at our house. We cleaned like we were preparing for the Second Coming, clicked on the A/C for the second time since moving to the park, and even waxed the avocado-green floors in the kitchen. Piles of mail were neatly stacked and dropped into a shoebox to be dealt with later.

Outside, a red Ferrari roared through the park, carefully clearing the speed bumps, and stopped in front of Tom Seman's lot—stealing the spot where his green Pinto was normally parked.

Keeping the sale of the park under wraps was now rendered impossible after he rolled up in a sports car that was worth more than $200,000.

A handsome man with thick, jet-black, wavy hair like David Hasselhoff strolled confidently to our office door. Thomas Saviano wore a deep-blue, shimmery suit, skinny black tie, and a Rolex.

My sister and I were enamored by this man, who looked like he'd walked off the set of *Knight Rider*. My little brother was obsessed more with his copper-plated beeper that was the size of today's smartphones and twice as thick.

My whole family gushed over his sports car and walked out following dinner to get a look inside. Tom appeared agitated and put our buyer on notice that he had taken his parking spot, all the while waiting for my parents to intervene. Thomas was polite and apologetic. We later had one of our many laughs over the years at Tom's expense after he chewed out his new landlord.

Summer was coming, and, for the next couple of weeks, we were kept busy with the prospect of finally getting out of here and enjoying a somewhat normal life. In addition to preparing the house for sale, finalizing commercial real estate was trickier and more time consuming than actually selling a house because you had to consider the tenants as well. Excitement was in the air, and I had never seen my parents less stressed or happier than during those few months.

My dad had even found a job outside of the park and had started a good year before we moved. Grandma refused to go house hunting with us especially when we started looking in the Carrollwood development.

My parents eventually ruled out the community after many discussions and sparring with Grandma.

One month later, we officially inked the sale on the park and moved into a trailer in Gibsonton, Florida, where the story continues …